THE COMPLETE BOOK OF MAN-TO-MAN OFFENSE

John Kresse
Richard Jablonski

COACHES CHOICE

ISBN: 1-57167-251-6
Library of Congress Catalog Card Number: 98-86164

Interior Design: Michelle A. Summers
Cover Design: Dody Bullerman
Front Cover Photo: Patrick Murphy-Racey
Diagrams: Mariah L. Oxford

Coaches Choice Books is a division of: Sagamore Publishing, Inc.
                                           P.O. Box 647
                                           Champaign, IL 61824-0647
                                           Web Site: http//www.sagamorepub.com

DEDICATION

To our families:

John, Ryan and Sue Sommer-Kresse,

and Christian and Pat Ring-Jablonski.

ACKNOWLEDGMENTS

The authors wish to acknowledge those coaches, players and observers of basketball who have influenced their careers and contributed concepts and ideas to this book.

For John Kresse, there are too many to mention individually. But no such list would be complete without his former coach at St. John's University, Joe Lapchick, and his fellow coach at St. John's and with the New York Nets, Lou Carnesecca. Kresse also recognizes the collective impact and contribution of the many assistant coaches and players he has worked with during 19 years at the College of Charleston.

For Richard Jablonski, professional influences include those journalists in New York and elsewhere whose writing he still studies and enjoys. His career path in writing is largely the responsibility of his father, Edward T. Jablonski, who never failed to bring home a newspaper at the end of the day.

Also, the authors appreciate the work of many people at Sagamore Publishing and Coaches Choice Books, including Jim Peterson, Michelle Summers and Mariah Oxford.

CONTENTS

FOREWORD

One of the great joys of coaching basketball is the many people you get to meet and know through the game. Nearly 40 years ago, when I was an assistant coach under the legendary Joe Lapchick at St. John's University, I met John Kresse. It didn't take long for me to see that this kid was an incredibly hard worker who loved the game of basketball. So I asked him, "Would you like to get involved in coaching?" That summer, John went to Clair Bee's camp, the granddaddy of all basketball camps. I think that's where he really started to get involved.

John took his first job in 1964 at Christ the King High School in New York. A year later, when Coach Lapchick retired from St. John's and I was fortunate enough to succeed him, I asked John to join me as one of my assistants. It's a great story. The first game I ever coached at St. John's was the freshmen against the varsity. John took the freshmen and beat me. He felt so bad he wouldn't come to practice the next day. That was the start of a long professional relationship. John was my assistant for the next 14 years—11 with St. John's and three with the New York Nets of what was then the American Basketball Association.

In 1979, John left St. John's for the College of Charleston, where he has enjoyed nothing but success on and off the court. He has a wonderful family, a marvelously successful basketball program, and a loyal following of thousands of Charlestonians. Among his peers, he is regarded as one of the top coaches in the college game—a man with a keen eye for basketball and the ability to translate that vision into a remarkable winning percentage on the court. He and his team are no longer two of the best-kept secrets in college basketball.

None of this surprises me. You could tell at an early age that John was a real student of the game. He always had a certain flair for basketball. Sometimes, you can develop that in a person, but in John's case, you could see it was more than that. It was inherent. You can see that John still has a special feel for the game by the way he handles situations. A lot of people can learn basketball from a book. But to be really successful, you must have a feel for the game. John has that gift.

John's whole life is dedicated to basketball. His love for the game is reflected in this book about man-to-man offense—a book which, combined with his previous book on zone offense, provides a valuable resource for coaches at all levels.

> Lou Carnesecca
> Former Head Coach, St. John's University
> 1992 Inductee, Naismith Memorial Basketball Hall of Fame, Springfield, MA

HOW THIS BOOK WILL HELP YOUR PROGRAM

During more than three decades as a basketball coach at the high school, college and professional levels, I have witnessed many changes in the game I love. The sheer athleticism of players at all levels is at times astonishing. Thirty-five years ago, you could count the players with the power and grace of Elgin Baylor on two hands and still have a couple of fingers left over. Nowadays, it seems as though every time I look out on the court during a College of Charleston game, I see 10 players with speed, quickness, power, leaping ability or, in some cases, all four of those athletic traits. The game is routinely played at a faster pace and above the rim.

This having been said, certain things about the game not only haven't changed; they're even more central to a team's success. First and foremost among these is defense—especially man-to-man defense. At a time when more and more players are offensive threats, and average perimeter shooters score points three at a time, the ability to play man-to-man defense hard and well is paramount. At the professional level, man-to-man defense is the rule. At the college level, it may as well be, considering how many teams play it on a full-time basis.

Yes, there are exceptions. Temple Coach John Chaney is renowned for his commitment to zone defense. Many successful programs include zone defense in their bag of tricks. At the College of Charleston, we mix match-up zone in with our man-to-man, depending on time, score, individual match-ups and foul trouble. We believe the ability to change defenses contributes greatly to our success. However, when the chips are down, especially when trailing, we rely heavily on man-to-man defense to produce the results we need.

This strategy puts us among the vast majority of teams at the college level and an increasing number of high school teams. I am hard-pressed to recall the last time one of our opponents played 40 minutes of zone defense against us. Certainly, it hasn't happened during the last three or four seasons. During the 1996-97 season, we played 62 games, against the likes of Arizona, Kentucky, Stanford, Maryland, Oklahoma State, Arizona State and Massachusetts. Every team we faced, big or small, played some man-to-man against us. Some teams played man-to-man exclusively. The teams that played a lot of zone often used a match-up philosophy, incorporating many man-to-man principles in their zones.

There is no single explanation for this phenomenon. Certainly, the presence of a shot clock and a makeable three-point shot has affected the game's strategy. Ask yourself, why concede open shots to an opponent pressed for time by a shot clock? Why allow a strong shooting team to launch uncontested three-point shots over a zone? The answers to these questions point to a man-to-man defensive philosophy.

Time and score also determine defensive strategy. When trailing late in a game and time is your greatest enemy, you can't afford to let an opposing team milk critical seconds from the clock by passing the ball around the perimeter of a zone. When leading by two or three points late in a game, you'll probably want to play man-to-man defense to contest, rather than concede, a potential tying or winning shot from the perimeter.

The success of programs like Duke and Indiana also contributes to the prevalence of man-to-man defenses. Coaches Mike Krzyzewski at Duke and Bob Knight at Indiana have collected multiple national titles in large part due to the stinginess of their teams' man-to-man defenses. This certainly gives coaches—collectively some of the greatest copycats you'll ever meet—reason to install man-to-man defenses in search of Duke-like results.

But, none of that matters when the game is on the line and your opponent is playing man-to-man defense. That's when you face the bottom line. You might as well face it now. If your team can't attack man-to-man defenses systematically and effectively, it won't win as many games as it should. If you're going to develop a consistent winner at any level, from grade school to pro, men or women, your team must be able to attack man-to-man defenses.

At the College of Charleston, we have installed a multi-faceted system that incorporates elements of inside and outside offense to attack and defeat man-to-man defenses in the halfcourt setting. We present that system in this book for those coaches who want to take their teams to the highest possible level. I want to help you get the job done.

Take the correct approach, and your offense will consistently produce high-percentage shots. You can free up your top scoring threats where they can do the most damage. You can create exciting isolation opportunities to take advantage of individual mismatches. You can enable offensive rebounders to anticipate shots, work for prime rebounding position and score stick-back baskets.

Make no mistake about it, man-to-man defense has come a long way in recent decades. With the help of videotape scouting and an evolving understanding of the game, coaches have become increasingly sophisticated in their strategies, fine-tuning their defenses to stymie high-scoring opponents. Sagging, helping defenses take away inside opportunities. Overplaying, double-teaming defenses pressurize shooters and ballhandlers. But no defensive team can do all things on every possession. Each concedes openings to a well-schooled team. The trick is taking advantage of those opportunities through rigorous preparation and game-time execution.

This book is about preparation, which leads to execution.

If your players are prepared to handle everything a defense shows, if they know they have a specific, tactical response to every situation, they will play with the confidence and peace of mind needed to dissect stingy defenses. Ultimately, they will put the defending team on the defensive, not only physically, but strategically and emotionally. Through their effectiveness on the offensive end, your players will force opposing players and coaches to make difficult, often incorrect choices. In an ideal situation, you may force an opposing coach to get away from what his team does best and switch to an alternative defensive strategy. As a coach, you know this seldom works.

The following chapters contain elements of what has worked for some legendary coaches: Clair Bee, Nat Holman, Joe Lapchick, Lou Carnesecca, Red Holzman, John Wooden and Denny Crum, among others. In my years as a player for Lapchick at St. John's University, and as an assistant to Carnesecca at St. John's and with the New York Nets of the American Basketball Association, I was blessed with the opportunity to meet, listen to and observe some of the game's great minds. I learned a lot of basketball watching fellow coaches frantically moving furniture around an office to simulate game situations. I did a great deal of learning at dining tables, where salt and pepper shakers were put to offensive and defensive tasks and napkins were used to create now-famous diagrams.

And then, there was the actual game experience—whether coaching or watching. This book presents an evolving philosophy and outlook, as I learn more and more about the game by coaching against the likes of Gary Williams at Maryland and Lute Olson at Arizona. In the second round of the 1997 NCAA Tournament, the College of Charleston faced Olson and his eventual national champions, Arizona. The Wildcats got the better of us, 73-69, but not before I had the privilege of coaching in a classic battle between two teams with diverse, well-schooled, man-to-man offenses. As many plays as we called, it seemed as though Coach Olson called just as many, or more. That experience, and Arizona's subsequent march to a national championship, reinforced my strongly held belief that access to a comprehensive man-to-man system is a must for success at the highest level of college and professional basketball.

What about other levels? I know that coaches at the high school level simply don't have the practice time and staff support to install every concept and play presented in this book. Who does? In any given year, we incorporate all major elements presented here, but certainly not every play and wrinkle. Each coach must evaluate his program's needs and resources. As a coach, you must prioritize. If you need a set-play offense, it's here. If you're looking for a breakdown offense, it's here. Special situations? Covered. Basic principles? Right here. Use this book to improve your program in those areas where you need work. Pick and choose those plays and concepts that mirror your philosophy, resources and beliefs.

Fundamental beliefs are a big part of any successful program. I know all games are won or lost on the court, but every coach should be a little bit of a dreamer. I hope this book encourages you to think about the game—to daydream a little—and gives you the tools to fulfill those dreams on the court.

John Kresse
College of Charleston

CHAPTER 1

Basic Principles: Rules to Win By

Over the course of my career, I have collected and refined a list of basic principles for attacking man-to-man defenses in the halfcourt setting. Some of these principles are strategic; others deal with technique; still others are philosophical in nature.

There's no mystery to the fact that the best way to attack any halfcourt defense— man or zone—is by outrunning it. The most successful teams install, practice and refine their fastbreak attacks, knowing when and how to push the ball upcourt to their greatest advantage. I'll leave it up to each coach to install his or her fastbreak attack. This book is about what your team should do when the break is not available and the players settle into a halfcourt chess match.

Here, then, are 12 basic principles for attacking man-to-man defenses in the halfcourt setting. Study these principles. Incorporate them into your thinking and teaching. They'll help you understand material presented in subsequent chapters, and they'll give you and your players a foundation upon which to develop a potent man-to-man offense.

RECOGNIZE THE DEFENSE

Yes, some teams play nothing but man-to-man defense. Others play nothing but zone. In those cases, recognizing an opponent's defense is a fairly straightforward matter, even though you'll still want possession-by-possession confirmation that nothing has changed.

But what about those opponents who play a variety of defenses? Even more complex, what do you do when an opponent initially shows one defense, then plays another?

Clearly, when facing a team that runs multiple defenses, you and your team must quickly "crack the code." By this, I mean you must recognize the opponent's defense, call an appropriate play, organize for the play, then run it. For now, let's work on the initial issue: recognizing the defense. It's not always as easy as it sounds.

One way to recognize and prepare for specific defenses is by scouting. If you have the manpower and time to scout future opponents, you can gain a substantial edge. Rather than waiting for the game to begin and making a trip downcourt to determine what defense an opponent is playing, scouting allows you to observe and prepare for specific defenses in advance. Chances are, an opposing coach will use many of the same defenses from game to game because he has tailored his defensive gameplan to his players' skills. Those skills don't change from game to game. Whatever small refinements he makes in his defensive gameplan will be dictated by your team's individual and collective skills on the offensive end. You may be sure that, whatever your team does best, your opponent will try to stop, or at least contain it.

While scouting is a valuable tool, it doesn't take the place of a well-trained eye, especially when the scouting trip reveals that your future opponent uses both man-to-man and zone defenses. Man-to-man defense is just that—an individual defender is responsible for an attacking player, one-on-one, all over the court. In zone defenses, defenders match up with attacking players within a prescribed area or section of the court.

Most of the time, you'll be able to tell by simple observation whether your opponent is playing man-to-man defense. On those occasions when you have a doubt, run a man-to-man set play and observe your opponents' reactions. If a defender follows a cutter from one side of the floor to the other, chances are pretty good that you're facing a man-to-man defense.

There are exceptions to this general rule. As defenses have evolved, more and more teams play aggressive, match-up zone defenses. Most match-ups deploy defenders in areas where the offense originates. For example, if your offense originates from a 1-3-1 set, the defense will take on a 1-3-1 look. This can be confusing to the untrained or less experienced eye. Don't be discouraged. In theory, you can run your man-to-man offense against a match-up zone. We occasionally do this at College of Charleston as another means of promoting the kind of ball and player movement we need to defeat match-up zones.

Also, be alert for combination defenses, such as the box-and-1, the diamond-and-1 and the triangle-and-two. These defenses combine elements of man-to-man and zone defense—deploying three or four players in zone defense, with the remaining players matched up man-to-man.

STUDY OPPONENTS' TENDENCIES

At the risk of oversimplifying, different teams play the same defense differently. One team's sagging, inside-oriented, man-to-man defense presents a substantially different challenge than another team's hyperactive, overplaying defense. Yes, both are playing man-to-man, but each concedes unique opportunities to the attacking team.

As you observe your opponents' individual and team defensive skills, whether on a scouting mission or during a game, take mental notes and try to answer the following questions:

- How aggressive and physical is your opponent on the defensive end?

  Some teams are very aggressive, overplaying perimeter players and passing lanes, or trapping ballhandlers with quick double-teams. These ploys imply one-on-one matchups inside, the opportunity for perimeter players to move to the basket with and without the ball, and open shooters on the weak side of the floor (away from the ball). Players off the ball must be prepared to move to outlet positions to help a double-teamed teammate. Conversely, some teams prefer to take away inside play with sagging defenses. Your inside players must be aware of potential double-teams by perimeter defenders. When this occurs, perimeter shooters must step into high-percentage spots on the floor and look for inside-out passes.

- Does your opponent sustain a consistently strong defensive effort throughout each possession, and from possession to possession?

  In this book, I'll detail two approaches to attacking man-to-man defense—the quick-hitting set play and the breakdown offense. If the set play doesn't produce a high-percentage shot, we reset into a breakdown offense that uses as many passes and screens as time allows to produce an offensive opportunity. Many of our best looks come late in a shot clock when an opposing team or player fails to sustain a high intensity level and concentration. At the high school level, where there is no shot clock, if you're well-schooled and handle the ball well, you can force an opponent to sustain an effort for minutes at a time.

- How well do opposing players help each other, if at all?

  Despite its name, man-to-man defense is a team proposition. The best man-to-man defenses work as a unit, with all four players off the ball prepared to help a teammate should he be beaten by a strong one-on-one move. Attacking players must understand that effective helping defenses concede open shots with one or two more passes. Also, attacking players must be prepared to come to a jump stop to avoid charging calls. The jump stop and pass and the quick pull-up jump shot are effective tools for attacking man-to-man defense.

- How well do your opponents play screens?

  Our man-to-man offenses generally incorporate a screen or series of screens to free up scorers for high-percentage shots. As you know, there are several ways for a defender to cope with a solid, well-timed screen. He can go over the top of the screener and his defender, go under the screener and his defender, or go between the screener and his defender. Well-schooled teams are consistent in their approach to defending against screens. Learn your opponents' tendencies and instruct your players accordingly. For example, should your opponents consistently go beneath screens, they may be vulnerable to jump shots in our breakdown offenses. On the other hand, a defender who always fights over a screen can be beaten by quick curl and backdoor moves. We'll talk more about these things as the book progresses.

For now, the important thing to know is that each team, whether by coaching philosophy, player skill or a combination of the two, plays its own unique brand of man-to-man defense. Answers to the questions posed here provide a coach with insight on game preparation and play-calling decisions.

EVALUATE MATCHUPS ON AN ONGOING BASIS

The basic building block of man-to-man defense is the individual matchup. At some point, your coaching opponent makes a decision or series of decisions regarding which player or players will match up, one-on-one, with the players you send out on the floor. Some of these decisions are simple, based on size and quickness issues. For example, your big man will most likely be covered by a big man, and your best perimeter threat will be covered by your opponents' most skilled perimeter defender. However, in virtually every man-to-man defense, there is some compromise. By this, I mean that your opponent may have a player or two on the floor for reasons other than defense. In Chapter 2 of this book, I'll get into some of the decisions all coaches face when putting a starting lineup on the floor. Of course, those decisions get even tougher as a game moves along and fatigue, foul trouble, injuries and other problems crop up.

As you look at individual matchups, be aware of each and every individual edge your players may have. In my experience, an edge in size, quickness, skill, experience, intensity or foul trouble can be decisive in an individual matchup. The outcome of a game often hinges on taking advantage of these individual matchup advantages.

If you have a size advantage at center, why not punch the ball inside to your big man? If one of your perimeter players has a decided edge in quickness, why not free him up for isolated one-on-one action? If one of your players has a hot hand, why not get him the ball? If one of your seniors is being guarded by a freshman, why not look to exploit the rookie's comparative inexperience for some easy baskets? If you see that an individual defender lacks intensity or concentration, why not take the ball right at him and see how he holds up? If an opponent is in foul trouble, why not force him to make the tough choice between letting up on defense or risking a disqualifying foul?

Understand that every game has its own ebb and flow. Matchups change, and along with them, individual advantages come and go. Try to think about every possible individual matchup your players will face before the ball goes up, and you'll be in much better position to make game-winning decisions during the heat of battle.

These decisions—some obvious, some intuitive—are yours to make as a coach. By installing set-play and breakdown offenses, you arm yourself with options for every situation.

KNOW YOUR OWN PLAYERS' STRENGTHS AND WEAKNESSES

In Chapter 2, I discuss the mix of physical skills and intangibles we look for when putting five players on the floor. As you'll see, balance is critical to success. In an ideal situation, your five players on the floor combine to offer dribbling, passing, scoring, rebounding and defensive skills. However, you seldom find a player who possesses all five skills.

As a coach, you'll achieve your greatest success by putting players in position to do what they do best. Our set-play and breakdown offenses do just that. We ask dribblers to dribble, passers to pass, and scorers to score. More importantly, we don't ask or expect players to do things they can not do. For instance, we don't expect or ask our big man to step away from the basket, catch the ball in triple-threat position, and pull up for a three-point shot. Instead, we create close-in opportunities for inside players, open jump shots for great shooters, and one-on-one opportunities for slashers.

Do these things consistently, and you'll improve your team's performance in several key areas: shooting percentage, assist-to-turnover ratio, and inside-outside balance. Success in these areas translates into success on the bottom line.

TIMING: FINDING AND HITTING OPENINGS

Suppose you have a 10 a.m. appointment to meet with a business client. Get there at 9:30, and you waste 30 minutes of your valuable time. Get there at 10:30, and chances are your client is already gone. Indeed, he may no longer be your client.

Timing is just as important in basketball. With split-second timing, you can find the player who will make the most effective finish after the proper pass and catch.

In our set-play offense against man-to-man defense, we generally look for one or two primary options. Timing is critical to the success of this kind of attack. The point guard—your coach on the court—must initiate plays only when his teammates are organized and ready to go. The first pass receiver—usually a wing player—must have the physical ability and understanding to free himself up at just the right time and place on the floor. From that moment, when the point guard initiates the play and makes that first pass, a set play should run like clockwork.

Because your initial set play won't always produce a high-percentage opportunity, your players must have the presence of mind to organize and initiate a breakdown offense in a timely fashion. This is particularly important at the college level, where the shot clock can determine the length of a possession. If you're working on a 35-second shot clock and use 15 seconds to initiate and run a set play, you're left with 20 seconds to organize and execute a breakdown offense. Don't get me wrong—20 seconds is plenty of time to do what needs to be done. Conversely, 10 seconds may not be enough time to produce a high-quality shot, so a few wasted seconds here and there can be costly. At the high school level, these situations come up at least four times a game at the ends of quarters. The team that executes well in time-critical situations often comes out a winner.

Some of this boils down to developing a correct time-space relationship between players and the ball. Proper spacing and timing are key elements in attacking man-to-man defenses. Ideally, we look for 12- to 15-foot spacing between attacking players, allowing each player the space and time to operate effectively, and reducing the number of long, looping, interceptable passes. Again, the point guard's initiation of the play and the wing player's positioning to catch the first pass will determine much of your players' space-time relationship on the floor.

It's important to understand that repetition is the key to developing the kind of timing you need to attack and defeat man-to-man defenses. By dummy and live work in practice, the interrelated efforts of each player become second nature. The team develops the cohesion to perform as a unit automatically. And that's critical. Once on the court, players can't afford to think about timing. It must be automatic.

THE POISE-PATIENCE PAYOFF

In our set-play and breakdown offenses, we rely on good execution to find and create openings for high-percentage shots. If our set play produces a high-percentage shot after one or two passes, fine. However, there is no guarantee that a set play, no matter how well-executed, will produce the kind of shot we want.

Give the defense some credit. Your opponent will take away some of your first-option, set-play chances with hard, aggressive play and anticipation. When this occurs, maturity and teamwork are keys. A mature, well-drilled team has the poise and patience to shift gears on the fly, get into a breakdown offense such as we'll describe later in this book, and continue to attack.

This is particularly important given some defenses' tendency to "let up" after a certain amount of time or number of passes. Even though they're built on one-on-one intensity, some man-to-man defenses fail to sustain a high level of effort. After

"X" number of passes, individual defenders lack aggressiveness and focus. Often, all you'll need is the patience to find the weak link: a player who lacks concentration and follow-through on the defensive end.

Some of our set plays are designed to produce a single scoring opportunity. Others offer options with a few more passes. In theory, our breakdown offenses may be run for however many passes are needed to produce a high-percentage shot.

When there is no shot clock, an offense can do whatever is necessary to produce a high-percentage scoring opportunity. But remember, even with the 35-second shot clock employed at the college level, there is usually plenty of time to rethink and reset. Thirty-five seconds can be an eternity, especially when you're trying to sustain an intense defensive effort.

DRIBBLING: THE WAY THE BALL BOUNCES

Whether initiating a play, executing a set play or breakdown offense, or taking advantage of one-on-one opportunities, the dribble is a critical element of successful man-to-man offense. Ideally, you want five players on the floor who can dribble the ball with varying levels of skill. Your guards must be able to dribble to initiate the offense. Your forwards must use the dribble to take advantage of scoring opportunities. Even your center should be able to dribble, though not necessarily at high speed in the open floor.

To begin, the dribble is very effective in initiating a set, halfcourt offense. We often initially take the ball away from the intended area of attack. Our thinking is that this ploy creates better passing lanes and negates an opponent's ability to use overplay or denial strategies. Quick ball reversal off the dribble occasionally catches a defense before it can react with an overplay.

Once you're into a set play or breakdown, your offensive execution will create a variety of dribble-drive opportunities for skilled players. We use the dribble drive most often from the wing or short-corner positions. These short bursts, whether all the way to the basket or for a pull-up jump shot, are most effective in that they occur before the beaten defender's teammates can react and help. Lengthier dribble drives give well-coached defenders time to react, step into the lane, and draw charging fouls. Remind your players of this possibility, and drill them on pulling up for jump shots in practice. See the opening and attack it, but don't play into the defense's hands by driving out of control. Drive with a purpose, but use control and vision to exploit a defense and make the most of the opportunity.

On the perimeter, a good hard dribble or two may be all it takes to improve an angle for a pass into the post. While teams that play full frontal defense in the post are rare, teams that try to establish at least a "halfway" position in defending the low post are fairly common. In this approach, the post defender works to get halfway around the attacking player on the low block. Whether the post defender is on the high side (away from the baseline) or the low side of the attacking player, a smart perimeter player may use the dribble to create a better angle for a pass away from the post defender.

Speaking of post play, a player with his back to the basket must be selective in using the dribble. Two reasons: Post players seldom are your most skilled dribblers, and defenders often look to double-team an unwary post player from the perimeter or blind side, using the element of surprise to steal the ball. While I certainly don't advocate overuse of the dribble in the low post, I've learned over the years to "never say never." A good, strong move, using the dribble, can be very effective, but players should be alert to quick double-teams by ballhawking defenders.

PASSING

For virtually every score, except for clearouts and rebound/stickbacks, a player makes a correct pass when the opportunity presents itself. All defenses are vulnerable to crisp, well-chosen passes. I encourage you to drill passing, then use your best passers to execute critical passing elements of set plays.

On the perimeter, I prefer the two-hand chest pass. It's quick, efficient and easy to teach. The two-hand chest pass travels faster than the bounce or alley-oop pass, and effective man-to-man offense requires execution with precision and speed.

The bounce pass can be effective when feeding the low or mid post. A player receiving a bounce pass usually has his knees bent and is in ideal position to turn or spin either way for a strong move to the basket.

The bounce pass can also be effective on the backdoor play, which often is available against overplaying, denying defenses. Such situations as a forward backdoor with a guard pass, a forward backdoor with a high-post pass, or a high-post cut with a low-post pass employ the bounce pass effectively.

Used wisely, the alley-oop pass can be very effective against man-to-man defense. We occasionally screen defenders to open up lob opportunities. I remind you that an effective lob pass need not be caught above the rim for a slam-dunk finish. A simple catch and layup will do. Again, I encourage you to drill these plays at length to determine which of your players have the skills needed to throw, catch and finish a lob pass.

Against aggressive, helping defenses, the crosscourt or "skip" pass is a valuable weapon. You'll notice that a help-oriented man-to-man defense often stations weakside defenders in the lane. A good skip pass can lead to an uncontested jump shot or a strong penetration move. The defender often rushes out to cover a potential shooter, only to concede a quick dribble drive for an easier shot or penetrating pass.

Finally, you don't always need to pass the ball to make effective use of passing. A good ball fake opens up dribbling, passing and shooting opportunities, on the perimeter and inside.

THE PASS RECEIVER AS TRIPLE THREAT

Now that we've discussed passing and its role in our man-to-man offenses, let's consider the role of the pass receiver as triple threat.

Whether an attacking player faces toward or away from the basket, he must be able to shoot, pass or drive upon receiving the ball. The triple-threat concept makes each offensive player a potentially dangerous weapon in our man-to-man attack. Of course, the good offensive player thinks "score" whenever he receives a pass. But if the defense reacts correctly, taking away the shot or drive, the offensive player must be prepared to pass. Indeed, in our set-play attack, the pass often is the first, best option.

First, let's look at the shot. In our system, a high-percentage shot from the perimeter is defined simply as an unforced shot with a player's established range. Some players have the arm and leg strength to shoot over defenders. In our system, many shooters facing the basket have the luxury of distance from the defense and time to set up.

A high-percentage shot inside may also be uncontested, although that's generally not the case. When well-defended, an interior shooter must be ready to make a strong or elusive move, or shoot over a defender, immediately upon catching the ball.

When the shot is not available on the perimeter, this may imply that a defender is looking to deny the pass receiver's jump shot. In this situation, the quick dribble drive can be a highly effective weapon. Again, the driver must be aware of helping defenders, and be willing to pull up for a jump shot or pass.

Within the context of our set-play and breakdown offenses, the pass receiver must also be aware of his various passing options, then have the vision and court sense to pick the right option in a given situation.

SHOOTING

Ultimately, your team must put the ball though the hoop, or the best execution imaginable will go for naught. Our set plays create clearly prescribed shots, while our breakdown offenses produce a predictable range and variety of shots. Under these circumstances, spot-up shooting drills are a must in practice. Design drills that maximize repetitions from those spots and areas where shots will naturally occur within your offensive system. Encourage players to take "game" shots—perfecting their existing repertoire, then gradually expanding it as their physical maturity and skills permit.

For now, let's look at a few areas on the floor that serve as excellent launch sites for high-percentage shots. In later chapters, you'll learn how to create openings for your players to take these shots.

The perimeter is a good place to start—not because you want to take nothing but jump shots, but rather because many man-to-man defenses place priority on taking away an opponent's inside game. Against defenses that choke off inside play, the jump shot is an ever-present option. The trick is to create high-percentage shots—good shots taken by good shooters.

On the perimeter, the top-of-the-key or down-the-middle shot is a good bet. More often than not, a good-shooting guard will connect from straight on. One reason: the rim and backboard will more readily accept shots that are a touch short or long.

The foul-line-extended area, three or four feet beyond the elbow, is another high-percentage area for guards. It offers the additional benefit of excellent angles and lanes for passes into the paint.

Shooting guards and forwards can make good use of the wing areas, which offer the triple option of shooting, passing the ball into the post, or passing it back to the top of the key. The corners, 18 to 20 feet from the basket, are familiar territory for forwards and shooting guards.

On the interior, the prime shooting areas are the high, mid and low posts. The high post can be a wonderfully productive spot for a big man with shooting and passing skills. Often, he'll be left alone by sagging defenders, creating wide open shots or easy passes to open teammates on either side of the floor. The mid-post area, a few feet up the floor from the low block, is a potential gold mine for a player who possesses a turnaround jump shot, jump hook or pure hook. The low post is a power position. I encourage you to school low-post players on several back-to-the-basket moves, including turnaround jump shots, power moves and pump fakes, supplemented by the occasional dribble.

One additional bonus: establish your inside players, get the ball into the post areas often enough, and you create real havoc for the defense. Many coaches school their perimeter defenders to swarm the low post when the ball goes inside. This creates excellent "inside-out" opportunities, with the post player passing to a perimeter player for an uncontested jump shot.

OFFENSIVE REBOUNDING: THE EDGE

Offensive rebounding is a high priority in our man-to-man attack, and it should be in yours. The more opportunities you can generate through strong rebounding, the more likely you are to win the game. You might be surprised how often the team that out-rebounds its opponent on the offensive end wins the game.

But, how do you "manufacture" offensive rebounding? The answer, at the risk of oversimplifying, is by running an offense that produces shots at predictable places and times.

In our set plays—designed to produce a specific scoring opportunity—offensive rebounders have the tremendous advantage of knowing where and when shots will occur. Therefore, offensive rebounders can anticipate shots and maneuver inside defenders for optimum rebounding position.

In our breakdown offenses, we look for certain options that produce most of the shots. Once again, the advantage in anticipation is available. Because our breakdown offenses include a certain amount of ball and player movement from one side of the court to the other, prospective offensive rebounders must maintain their concentration and be prepared at all times to gain a positional edge on ball reversal.

The logic here is obvious. By designing situations that produce high-percentage passing, dribbling and scoring opportunities, you inevitably improve your offensive rebounding. Don't get me wrong. Nothing is automatic. Offensive rebounding still requires a lot of hard, physical work. But, it's a lot easier with the numerical and anticipation advantages afforded by a well-schooled offense. By knowing where all of your players are located on offense, you can create three-on-two, two-on-one and one-on-zero rebounding advantages. And it's tough to beat a one-on-zero advantage, isn't it?

I encourage you to work hard on rebounding in practice, encouraging players not only in the physical part of the task, but in the mental side of offensive rebounding. Size, quickness and intensity are great. Throw in some constructive anticipation, and you can do some real damage on the offensive boards.

SCREENING: NOT JUST THE BIG GUYS...EVERYONE

When playing against a committed, well-schooled, man-to-man defense, your offensive system must incorporate a variety of picks and screens to generate scoring opportunities. Ball and player movement alone, while important elements of your offense, are not enough to defeat solid man-to-man defense.

Why make the defenders' job easy? Think of it this way: no defender enjoys fighting through a single screen, or series of screens, to stay with his defensive assignment.

Even the best man-to-man defenses include a couple of players who aren't physical enough or lack the court awareness necessary to fight through or avoid well-set screens. Even the best defenders find themselves screened some of the time. They'd better, because in all likelihood your opponents' top defenders will be playing shirt-to-shirt defense against your best scorers.

Unlike our zone attack, described in *Attacking Zone Defenses*, our man-to-man offense requires that all five players on the floor occasionally set screens. This means that you, as coach, must instruct all of your players, regardless of position, in the art and science of setting a legal screen. At the College of Charleston, we encourage our players to set screens as big and wide as possible. We set screens early to assure they are stationary and not illegal. We encourage our players to come to a jump stop when setting a screen. The key elements of a legal screen are timing and control. By quickly establishing the player to be screened, then moving no more than 10 feet to set the screen, we develop the desired control.

In reading this book, you'll see a range of screens and picks. We screen on the interior and perimeter, on and off the ball, from behind, diagonally, big for little and little for big. In other words, you may see a few wrinkles you haven't seen or used before. I encourage you to incorporate them into your attack as part of a well-rounded system to defeat man-to-man defenses.

CHAPTER 2

The Balanced Machine

Balance. Talk to a coach of any team sport and chances are, sooner or later, the conversation will touch on the concept of balance. A football coach wants offense and defense. Within his offense, he wants running and passing. Within his running game, he wants a guy who can pound inside for tough yards teamed with a speedster who can turn the corner outside. And, ideally, both backs can block and catch passes.

Balance within balance within balance within balance. Give me that kind of balance, the coach will tell you, and he'll win the Super Bowl. Basketball offers similar rewards for balance. Balanced teams win games, and they have a lot of fun doing it.

To my way of thinking, the perfect basketball team would feature five all-around players, all of whom could shoot the lights out, dribble circles around defenders, make the perfect pass to the open man, rebound like demons, run the floor, and, of course, play defense. Wouldn't it be nice to coach that kind of team? Unfortunately, there are only so many Michael Jordans, Scottie Pippens, Magic Johnsons, Larry Birds and Oscar Robertsons. You're blessed if you have one. Nobody—not even the Chicago Bulls—has five.

Because there are so few "complete" players, coaches must continually evaluate players and make tough choices. Joe Lapchick, a member of the original Celtics and my coach at St. John's University, had his own system of evaluating players. When evaluating guards, Coach Lapchick considered three areas: scoring, ballhandling and defense. If a guard could do one of those three things well, he'd struggle for playing time. With two skills, he'd play a lot. With three, he'd be outstanding.

When evaluating forwards and centers, Coach Lapchick's criteria were scoring, rebounding and defense. Again, two skills made for an effective player, while three foreshadowed stardom.

In my years as a high school, college and professional coach, I've tried Coach Lapchick's system, and it works.

How does this affect the "balanced machine"? To be a consistent winner at any level, you must have the necessary components both offensively and defensively. Because this book illustrates offensive play, I won't dwell on defensive skills, other than to say that every team needs two or three strong individual defenders to win.

Stoppers in the backcourt and up front are necessities. Keep this in mind when evaluating players' offensive skills and contributions. All offensive skills being equal, go with the defensive stopper. Depending on the situation, give thought to going with the skilled defender even if his offensive skills don't quite match another player's weapons.

POSITION BY POSITION

Here's what we look for from each position on the court.

Point Guard

In our halfcourt offense, the point guard combines elements of court savvy, communication, ballhandling, shooting and defense. Before anything else, the point guard, in conjunction with the coach, must recognize the type of defense the opponent is playing, then communicate verbally or by hand signal the set play or breakdown offense we want to run. Once that's done and his teammates are in position, the point guard initiates the offense off the pass or dribble. The point guard should be a strong dribbler and a good passer, with some ability to penetrate and create scoring opportunities in the right situation.

With all of these responsibilities, the point guard isn't a primary scoring threat. But this player's ability to step in and hit the occasional jump shot goes a long way toward keeping sagging man-to-man defenses honest. A point guard who can hit the occasional jump shot prevents perimeter defenders from "diving in" to double-team low-post players.

The point guard should think defense while on offense. Should a shot be missed or an errant pass be thrown, someone must protect the backcourt. From a position on the perimeter, the point guard is a logical candidate for this duty.

Shooting Guard

The point guard's backcourt partner, often referred to as the shooting guard, should live up to that name. Unless challenged by a good shooter or two, most defenses will sag or collapse to deny a team's inside offense. The shooting guard, also occasionally called the off guard, should make perimeter defenders pay for helping their teammates inside. Ideally, he should be able to spot-shoot from the perimeter and slash aggressively to the basket on the dribble.

Recognizing the shooting guard's skills, many teams will overplay him, particularly in high-percentage shooting areas. When this occurs, an effective system of set-play and breakdown offense will be critical to your success. We help our shooting guard get open with a variety of picks, screens and ball reversals. It's up to the player to take advantage of the openings our offensive system creates.

The ability to dribble the ball to create scoring opportunities is vital. Many man-to-man defenses employ a "strongside-weakside" strategy, with weakside defenders sagging off their men. On quick ball reversal, defenders scramble to recover. Should a defender lose control in this situation, a clever shooting guard will exploit the opportunity for a quick drive, resulting in a layup, a pull-up jump shot or a pass.

In evaluating players for these positions, we have other considerations: rebounding and defense. We like to send our shooting guard to the offensive boards, especially if our opponent doesn't employ a fast-breaking, transition-minded offense. Should our opponent try to run, the shooting guard must have the quickness and presence of mind to sprint back and cover the backcourt.

Think of the point guard and shooting guard as a tandem, offering the right mix of court generalship, ballhandling, perimeter offense and defense—in a word, balance.

Small Forward

Balance is also important at the two forward positions. One of the forwards, usually the smaller and quicker of the two, should be competent from the perimeter as a shooter and passer. Like the shooting guard, he should be an accomplished spot shooter, usually from the wing and corner areas. Also, the small forward should be able to move effectively without the ball and possess an effective one-on-one game.

Our set-play and breakdown offenses create excellent opportunities for the small forward. Again, screening and picking free up the small forward for jump shots, "curl" moves, backdoor cuts and dribble drives.

We always go to the offensive boards with three big players. The small forward should get his share of offensive rebounds due to quickness and maneuverability, combined with the anticipation factor inherent in our set-play and breakdown offenses.

Power Forward

While the small forward assumes perimeter responsibilities, the other forward's strength should be just that—strength. Look at the way the game has evolved, and you'll understand what I'm saying. Players are getting bigger and stronger by leaps and bounds. Nowadays, it seems like every team we face has a power forward who is 6'7" and 230 pounds, minimum. This evolution is seen at all levels, with inside players a few inches taller, a few pounds heavier, and a few inches thicker in terms of muscularity.

This is not to say that your power forward should be a one-dimensional bruiser. It's great if your power forward can double as an outside threat, hitting an occasional 15-17-foot jump shot, combined with the occasional drive. But the power forward's primary offensive skills are posting up, setting and using screens, and rebounding.

In summary, the power forward is your team's blue-collar worker, performing a lot of tough, thankless tasks. If the small forward provides flash, the power forward provides crash. Again, balance.

Center

A complete center is tough to find. If you don't think so, just look around the National Basketball Association. Even at the game's highest level, there's only a handful of do-it-all centers.

In our man-to-man offenses, the center is a scorer, screener, rebounder and occasional passer. We drill our centers and power forwards on a variety of back-to-the-basket moves. When it comes to scoring, these are the center's bread and butter.

Once a center develops a back-to-the-basket repertoire, defenses will sag and double-team to reduce both the number of times he touches the ball and his effectiveness once he does catch it. This creates inside-out opportunities, in which the center must be able to find and hit an open teammate on the perimeter with a timely, accurate pass.

Offensive rebounding and screening are musts.

The center's offensive skills are important, but may be outweighed by defensive factors. The true shot-blocking center is a rare and valuable commodity. If you have one on your team, don't talk yourself out of using him because of his offensive shortcomings. With hard work, you can develop an adequate offensive player. You can not create a great shot-blocker.

EVALUATION AND TESTING

I've told you what we look for. Now, how do we find it?

How do we know which players will be most effective against man-to-man defenses? Which guard has the unique package of skills to run the show? Which guard and forward have the perimeter shooting and passing skills to keep defenses honest? Who has the strength and persistence to play power forward? Do we have a true center? If not, who can fill that role?

Obviously, accurate evaluation and testing of players' skills make attacking man-to-man defenses a much simpler task. Some players are simply better suited to attacking man-to-man defenses, as opposed to zones. They have the combination of physical skills and mental toughness needed to crack even the most aggressive and committed man-to-man defenses. They "see" the defense—its strengths and its vulnerabilities. But, how do you uncover these skills?

Start from scratch. By dummying (drilling without defense), we work on fundamentals and maneuvers in one-on-zero, two-on-zero and three-on-zero situations. Tell and teach your players what must be done, then show them how to do it. Make sure your players do what you ask. All successful coaches insist on execution at all levels and all times, beginning with practice.

After dummying, work against live defense. First, see how your players fare in one-on-one situations. Then expand your scope to the overall team picture. Look for examples of two-man and three-man basketball. Do your players "see" the game? Can they read defenses? Are they physical enough to win tough battles with the game on the line? Do they execute?

In tryouts, put your players through these basic situations, giving them every benefit of the doubt. Take and give as much time as you can afford. If you start and finish with a single scrimmage, you may overlook a player whose raw talent didn't shine through in a particular setting. Don't expect to see a bunch of complete players, and don't judge solely by a player's bottom-line productivity in a single game. As a coach, a big part of your job is discovering players' innate abilities, then developing and combining those skills into an effective unit.

Certain tools are particularly handy when attacking man-to-man defenses. One-on-one offensive skills obviously are paramount. But don't overlook a pure, spot-up shooter—a guy who can light up sagging defenses with perimeter jumpers. Having a specialist or two on hand at key times can be the difference between victory and defeat.

THE VALUE OF SITUATIONAL DEPTH

Throughout this chapter, I have used the word "balance" repeatedly, often in the phrase "the balanced machine." As everyone knows, no machine can function long-term without spare parts. In some cases, it's difficult to distinguish which parts are the spares and which are the originals. They're interchangeable.

Think of your car. During the summer, it rolls on standard-tread tires. During the winter, when faced with different road conditions, you may replace the regular tires with snow tires. Same machine. Different parts. Same results. You get where you're going.

Basketball coaches face changing conditions from game to game, often from minute to minute. So why not change parts to achieve maximum performance?

This is where your bench comes into play. Ideally, you'll have a minimum of eight effective players, if only to give starters an occasional breather, or to fill in when injuries or foul trouble strike. You should work to develop three guards, three forwards and two centers you can use with the game on the line. This is one kind of depth, and it's an absolute must.

The other kind, situational depth, is equally important. Situational depth goes beyond giving starters a breather. Situational depth gives a coach the flexibility to adapt to changing conditions on the floor. Let's say your opponent comes out in man-to-man defense. Early in the game, your players establish their ability to attack the defense for high-percentage scoring opportunities. Sensing this, the opposing coach switches to a zone defense, negating some of your one-on-one and power advantages, while conceding perimeter jump shots. Wouldn't it be nice to have an effective jump shooter, a real zone-buster, waiting on the bench for such an opportunity? The zone-buster may not be a complete player. He or she may not even be a major roleplayer. But a zone-buster certainly comes in handy when you need to loosen up a zone.

That kind of substitution works the other way, too. It may just be that, lurking on your bench, you have a one-dimensional, but potent, one-on-one scorer. What a great player to bring off the bench when you need firepower against a man-to-man defense. One player who comes to mind in this role is Cazzie Russell of the great New York Knicks teams in the 1960s and early '70s. Hall-of-Famer and former senator from New Jersey Bill Bradley was the Knicks' starter at small forward. And deservedly so, because Bradley possessed an array of offensive and defensive skills. But when Bradley needed a breather or the Knicks needed some quick points, Coach Red Holzman had a wonderful option in Russell. Cazzie was "instant offense."

A few other specialists to consider when developing your team's depth: a great ballhandler and foul shooter for end-game situations, a three-point shooter, and a great defensive stopper to put out the fire when an opponent's top gun heats up.

In developing depth, think of your players position by position. If you could, you'd have four guards—two point guards and two shooting guards. More likely, you'll have three guards. If that's the case, one must be able to play both positions.

Up front, you'd like four forwards and two centers—two players for each of the three distinct positions. As a minimum, you'll need three players capable of playing forward and two who can play center. For example, your starting power forward may be your backup center. You may find yourself substituting a small forward for a center, with your remaining forwards sliding over to other positions.

It's a bit of a chess game. The more pieces you have, the more likely you'll win. The player who can fill two positions effectively makes your job much easier.

One thing is certain. To attack man-to-man defenses with great success, you'll need a unit that combines elements of dribbling, passing, screening, jump shooting, inside scoring and rebounding—skills outlined previously in this chapter. Be aware that some of those skills may be sitting on your bench, just waiting to be turned loose when the situation arises.

CHAPTER 3

Planning Each Trip Downcourt

You've evaluated your personnel. You've discovered, as suggested in the previous chapter, that some players possess the unique skills and temperament needed to dissect zone defenses, while others are better suited to attacking man-to-man defenses. Indeed, depending on your team's depth, there probably is some overlap between the two groups. They may even be identical.

Regardless, you know the weapons at your command. Now's the time—preferably before the game—to think about the other guy. What is your opponent trying to accomplish defensively, and how does he go about doing it?

THINGS THE COACH MUST KNOW

To attack any man-to-man defense effectively, you must know its general tendencies, and how those tendencies translate into strengths and weaknesses on the floor.

Some defenses start tough and stay tough. Others don't sustain a high level of intensity and execution for more than five or six passes. Some defenses overplay perimeter ballhandlers and shooters, conceding backdoor and inside opportunities. Others sag and double-team inside, taking away interior passing and shooting, but opening up perimeter shooters. Some teams are well-schooled and consistent in defending against picks and screens; others are not. Some do a great job on the defensive boards; others do not. Do players on the opposing team communicate well on the defensive end? Do they help each other?

Individual tendencies are just as important. In my experience, very few teams will come at you with five great individual defenders. As you know, a coach's personnel decisions reflect players' skills at both ends of the court and in all phases of the game. In some instances, a coach will opt for a scorer over a solid one-on-one defender. He's conceding weakness at one end of the floor for strength at the other. A well-schooled man-to-man offense takes advantage of opponents' shortcomings in individual matchups.

Know your opponent's tendencies as well as your own and you gain a tremendous advantage. Aside from scouting, the best way to reveal an opponent's strengths, weaknesses, intentions and strategies is by running a variety of set plays and breakdown offenses early in the game. You and your staff should observe the result of each trip down the floor, then verify your observations with the help of statistics and shot charts.

Are you banging the ball inside effectively? Stats and shot charts should help you. Are you clicking at a high percentage from the perimeter? Again, stats and charts should answer your question.

Spend the early part of the game gathering information, then put that information to good use at crunch time. Check your ammunition and your top guns won't jam when they have to get off a game-winning shot.

SET PLAYS AND BREAKDOWN OFFENSES: WHICH AND WHEN?

We employ two basic approaches to attacking man-to-man defenses in a halfcourt setting—the set play and the breakdown.

Let's start with the set play. As the preseason progresses, we install as many as 15 set plays against man-to-man defense. These plays originate from a variety of offensive sets: 1-2-2, 1-3-1, Stack, and High 2-3 (described in later chapters). We gear each set play to go to one or two players. With a clearly prescribed and thoroughly practiced series of ball and player movements, we quickly produce a high-percentage shot for a specific player at a specific time and place. It follows, then, that set plays give you the opportunity to create specific opportunities for your most gifted scorers.

Just as your primary scorers fill a role, other players have roles to fill in a set play scheme. You need good passers and screeners to make set plays work. These roleplayers must understand the importance of what they do within the team framework. They must know their abilities and recognize their teammates' unique skills. As a coach, you can help players understand their roles by providing individual and team statistics. Properly employed, stats tell players not only what they've done, but what they're capable of doing to help the team.

Once players recognize and accept their roles, the set play is a truly effective way of attacking man-to-man defenses. You pinpoint the defense's weakness, whether individually or as a unit, and attack that weakness. A well-executed set play is like a successful surgical procedure. It's swift, clean and precise.

We always call a set play after our opponent makes a field goal or makes or misses a foul shot. After a missed field goal or a turnover, if we don't have a fast break opportunity, we call a set play. We also call set plays after violations or timeouts. We don't call set plays at the end of a fast break, preferring our secondary break, Motion or Flex-Plus offenses at that point. This avoids confusion and time lost while resetting to certain positions, and minimizes our vulnerability to a five-second count.

All of this having been said, you must understand that set plays are not the only way to attack man-to-man defenses. For example, let's say the defense does a great job diagnosing and stopping your set play. Or, your team attempts a fast break attack, only to pull the ball back out. What then?

At that point, we reset into one of two breakdown offenses—a passing game attack we call Motion, or a flex-style attack we call Flex-Plus. We call one of our breakdown offenses Flex-Plus because we've added wrinkles and principles to the traditional flex to create more and better opportunities for our team. In theory, your team can forego a set play offense and enter directly into either of these breakdown offenses. I prefer to use them after attempting a set play, or when fast break and secondary break options have failed to produce a shot.

Other than the flexibility of having "Plan B" in place, what benefits do these breakdown offenses offer?

First, our breakdown offenses place all of our players in scoring positions—not just one or two. Second, though patterned and principled, these offenses are not predictable. Individual players have options, within the flow of the offense. Finally, breakdown offenses can be used as time-killing devices late in quarters, halves or games, simply by instructing players to pass X number of times before attempting a shot. This may be a particularly useful strategy at the high school level, where there is no shot clock.

The option of passing the ball a prescribed number of times before attempting a shot can also help you determine an opponent's willingness and ability to sustain a high level of effort on the defensive end. The longer you can force a defense to sustain its effort and execution, the more likely you are to find individual weaknesses that can be exploited at critical times in a game.

You also may force opposing players to make difficult decisions "on the go" regarding defensive emphasis—whether to sag inside, overplay the perimeter, or whatever. In my experience, when a team gets away from what it does best defensively or abandons its defensive gameplan, it loses more often than not.

To review, I believe that a well-prepared team will have all the weapons it needs to attack man-to-man defenses in the halfcourt setting by installing set plays and at least one breakdown offense. Under most circumstances, as described previously, we run a set play first, then reset into a breakdown offense. Even with the 35-second shot clock, we find that we have plenty of time on each possession to organize and run a set play, then reset into a breakdown offense, if needed.

ORGANIZATION OF PLAYERS

After trying to score from our fast break or press attack, we make the smoothest transition possible into our halfcourt man-to-man attack.

Because our point guard initiates our set play offense, we get the ball into his hands as quickly as possible. As explained previously, the point guard bridges the communication gap between coach and players. But, how and when do we communicate?

At times, we run a series of up to four set plays, called before the game or during a timeout. In those instances, we don't verbally call or physically signal the plays we are running.

I know what you're thinking. Can I count on my players to handle that kind of mental load in pressure situations? I've found that with repetition and hard work in practices and scrimmages, players can handle this load. Let me break it down for you. We start at the blackboard, diagramming plays and explaining players' roles. From there, we take a play to the court, where we "dummy" it without defense. Once our players understand the play and execute it correctly without defense, we put defenders on the floor. This represents a real challenge for your players—running a set play against a defense that not only knows the play, but knows when it's coming. When a set play works against those odds, you have established the level of offensive execution you'll need to be successful in games. Once you have reached this level, you can begin to call plays in sequence, as many as four at a time.

It's all part of attacking man-to-man defenses. Think of it this way: The ability to remember and execute four plays is every bit as important in attacking man-to-man defenses as are certain physical skills.

At other times, we call our set plays one at a time, as early as possible, often when retreating on defense. If not then, you can call a play when taking the ball out after an opponent's field goal, or when an opponent is shooting a foul shot. On our opponents' missed field goals—and we hope there are plenty of those—we call or signal our play as we bring the ball up in the backcourt. This early organization allows players a chance to think about and plan the trip downcourt.

Once our players know the call and are in proper position to start the play, the point guard initiates the play off the pass or dribble. But, just what is "proper position?"

The point guard plays a key organizational role here. Although he obviously can not see all things at all times, we like our point guard to understand where each of his teammates should be at the start of a play. If the point guard initiates a play with teammates out of position, he and we are doomed to failure. In an ideal world—where all point guards are seniors and "coaches on the floor"—the point guard can be a traffic cop. In the real world, each player must understand and execute his role without prompting. Again, practice.

Given proper spacing and timing, we prefer to start our set plays as close to the basket as possible. We like to have the initial pass catcher receive the ball in position for a high-percentage shot or pass—not 30 feet from the basket.

Of course, surprises occur, and your team must be prepared for sudden changes in defensive strategy or emphasis. Teams are changing defenses more than ever; double-teaming, overplaying the first pass, or trying to force the ball to one side of the court.

How do you combat these adjustments? Obviously, recognition and immediate communication and adjustment are keys. Players and coaches must see the defense and react accordingly. Appropriate adjustments include: a backdoor option to combat the overplay; coming back to a double-teamed player to create an outlet pass; circling when double-teamed; reversing the ball to the weak side of the floor and looking to score; and resetting to a breakdown offense.

CHAPTER 4

The UCLA Series, Charleston Style

During a phenomenal run of titles and near titles in the 1960s and '70s, Coach John Wooden's UCLA Bruins were the model of college basketball excellence. The thought of playing Coach Wooden's team struck fear into the hearts of many a coach and player, who knew that the Bruins not only dressed some of the best talent in the game's history—Lew Alcindor (Kareem Abdul-Jabbar), Bill Walton and a raft of others—but used that talent in ways many of us could only hope to duplicate. With their great players, fabulous coaching and aura of invincibility, Coach Wooden's UCLA team's lent new and frightening meaning to the term "execution."

Most of my experience with UCLA came from afar, either watching the Bruins on television or in person during the NCAA Tournament. However, during the 1968 Holiday Festival in Madison Square Garden, St. John's faced UCLA and Lew Alcindor in the championship game. As an assistant at St. John's, I had the opportunity to watch Lew Carnesecca prepare his Davids to take on Goliath. During practice, Carnesecca gave a defending player a broom to simulate Alcindor's phenomenal reach and shot-blocking abilities. Broom or not, UCLA defeated St. John's for the tournament championship.

Take my word for it, that was a great team. But that's a different story. For now, let's zero in on what made the Bruins tick offensively—Coach Wooden's system. Aside from its virtually untouchable legacy of NCAA championships, the most lasting impact of the great UCLA dynasty of the '60s and '70s is the so-called UCLA Offense. The most visible active example of UCLA-style offense is Coach Denny Crum's Louisville Cardinals. No surprise there. Coach Crum is, after all, a former assistant to Coach Wooden at UCLA. At Louisville, Coach Crum has put his own stamp on the UCLA Offense, riding it to two national titles and perennial success. Like his teacher, Denny Crum is a Hall-of-Fame coach.

In 1979, when I first took the job as head coach at the College of Charleston, I began to install elements of the UCLA Offense. Over the years, my assistants and I have developed and installed a series of effective UCLA options—16 in all—all originating from the same basic 1-3-1 set. The beauty of the UCLA offense the way we run it is that it incorporates the skills of all five players, generating unique scoring opportunities for each. It plays to each player's individual strengths. It forces defenders to make difficult, "no-win" decisions. Also, as you'll see later in this chapter, the offense can be run to either side of the floor, effectively doubling the number of looks it produces.

So, with a tip of the hat to Coach John Wooden, I present the UCLA Series, Charleston Style. For the purposes of this book, let's take a look at each of our 16 options, one at a time. I'll leave it up to you to devise a play-calling system, whether by number, letter or name. To make it more difficult for our opponents to recognize play calls, we typically assign each play a letter name (A, B, C, etc.) and a number. We also develop hand signals for certain plays and continuities.

At the end of this chapter, we detail a few special challenges players face in executing the UCLA offense.

OPTION NO. 1

Perhaps we should call this Options 1-A, 1-B, 1-C, 1-D and 1-E. In the space of five diagrams, you'll see a basket cut by the point guard, 1, a post-up by 1, a quick isolation for the power forward, 4, and a 3-for-1 screen.

Diagram 4-1: 1 initiates the offense with the dribble. 3 buries his defender and cuts to a wing area. The center, 5, flashes up the lane to the left elbow area. 1 passes to three.

Diagram 4-2: After passing to 3, 1 "shuffle" cuts to the basket on either side of a screen by 5. 3 looks for 1 for a layup or similar high-percentage scoring opportunity.

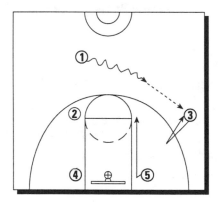

Diagram 4-1.

Diagram 4-2.

Diagram 4-3: Let's assume that 1's defender fights through the screen by 5 and denies the potential pass from 3 to 1. 5 steps out from the elbow area and establishes himself in triple-threat position for a pass from 3. 1 posts up for a possible pass from 5. 2 frees himself as an outlet on the weak side.

Diagram 4-4: 4 flashes into the lane from the weak side for a pass from 5. If 4 is overplayed or fronted, 5 may pass to 2, creating a better angle for a penetrating pass. At the same time, 3 screens for 1, moving to a wing area.

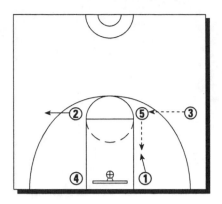

Diagram 4-3.

Diagram 4-4.

Diagram 4-5: 5 passes to 1 for a jump shot or a pass to 3 posting up.

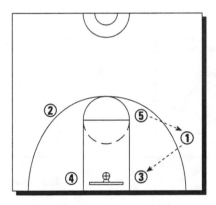

Diagram 4-5.

OPTION NO. 2

The primary goal here is to isolate 4 on the low block. Of course, should 1 be open on the initial cut, 3 can and should hit his teammate for a layup.

Diagrams 4-6 and 4-7: 1, 3 and 5 initiate the offense. On this play, when compared to Option No. 1, previously diagrammed, 2 and 4 are inverted. 2 starts near the right block. 4 starts near the right elbow.

Diagram 4-8: 3 passes to 5 and screens for 1. On the pass from 3 to 5, 4 screens for 2 and posts up. 5 passes to 2 at the right elbow or foul-line extended area.

Diagram 4-9: 2 takes an open jump shot or passes to 4, isolated in a low-post area.

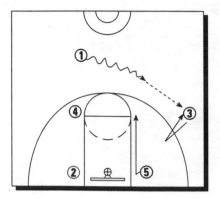

Diagram 4-6.

Diagram 4-7.

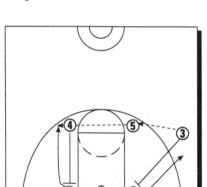

Diagram 4-8.

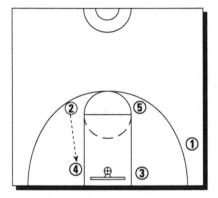

Diagram 4-9.

Diagram 4-10: Should 5 not be able to pass to 2, he can pass to 1 on the wing, setting up an open jump shot by 1 or a post-up opportunity for 3.

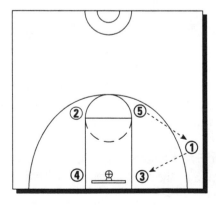

Diagram 4-10.

OPTION NO. 3

Is there any play more demoralizing to a defense and electrifying for an offense than a lob pass and dunk? Option No. 3 creates an opportunity for your 5 man to do what he does best—finish around the basket. This option also reemphasizes a point we made earlier about screening. As a coach, you must teach all of your players, big and small, how to set legal, effective screens. The point guard sets a key screen here.

Diagrams 4-11 and 4-12: 1, 3 and 5 initiate the offense. 4 sets up at the elbow area; 2 down low.

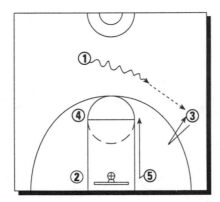

Diagram 4-11.

Diagram 4-12.

Diagram 4-13: 3 passes to 5, then clears, via the baseline, to the opposite side of the floor. 4 screens for 2.

Diagram 4-14: On the pass from 5 to 2, 1 screens up the lane, freeing up 5 for a lob pass from 2. Depending on the quality of the pass and 5's leaping ability, 5 can either catch and dunk or catch and lay the ball in the basket.

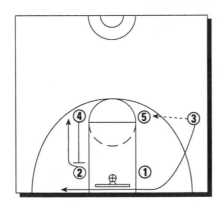

Diagram 4-13.

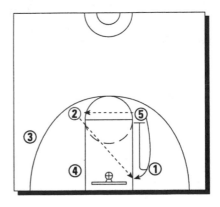

Diagram 4-14.

Diagram 4-15: A well-schooled defense may deny the 2-to-5 pass. Certainly, once a defense has seen this play, it's tougher to complete a second time. That's why 1, after setting a screen for 5, steps away from the elbow and faces the basket in triple-threat position. If need be, 2 can pass to 1, who may find 5 posting up against a defender who has overplayed and denied the initial lob threat.

Diagram 4-15.

OPTION NO. 4

When the defender on 1 consistently denies the basket cut and pass from 3, it's time to show him something different. This option allows 1 to fade off 5's screen for a jump shot, dribble penetration or pass to 5. In my years as coach, I've seen different point guards finish this play their own way, with a slashing move to the basket, a drive and pull-up shot, or a wide-open perimeter jump shot. All three are good options. In theory, you can run this play for a three-point shot.

Diagram 4-16: 1, 3 and 5 initiate the play as usual. On the pass from 1 to 3, 2 and 4 clear to the strong side (or ball side) of the floor, taking defenders with them.

Diagram 4-17: Instead of cutting all the way down the lane to the basket, 1 buries his defender, then uses a screen by 5 to free himself up in an area left of the key. After catching the pass from 3, 1 has passing and scoring options on the right side of the floor.

Diagram 4-18: As 1 looks to penetrate, 5 rolls into the lane for a scoring opportunity. 3 replaces 5, and 2 balances the floor.

Diagram 4-16.

Diagram 4-17.

Diagram 4-18.

OPTION NO. 5

This is a multi-option quick-hitter, creating excellent scoring opportunities for four players in the space of three or four passes.

Diagram 4-19: The play initiates with 1 passing to 3 and 5 establishing screening position at the left elbow area. On the pass from 1 to 3, 4 movers diagonally across the lane to replace 5 on the low left block.

Diagram 4-20: Instead of cutting off the screen by 5, 1 follows his pass to 3 for a hand-off. 3 then moves to the left baseline. 2 moves to a right-wing area.

Diagram 4-21: 5 steps away from the elbow area to set a strong dribble block in the foul-line extended area. 1 uses the dribble block to dribble penetrate to the foul line area. 1's options include a pull-up jump shot, a quick pass to 4 ducking into the lane, or the penetrate-and-kick pass to 2 on the wing.

Diagram 4-22: After setting the dribble block, 5 rolls to the right low block, looking for a layup or establishing post-up position for a pass from 1.

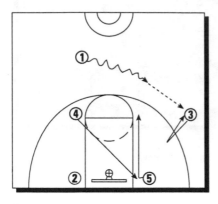

Diagram 4-19.

Diagram 4-20.

Diagram 4-21.

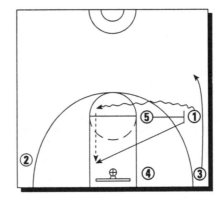

Diagram 4-22.

OPTION NO. 6

Remember, if you really want to see set-play offense at the highest level, watch National Basketball Association games live or on television. With very few exceptions—Doug Moe during his tenure with the Denver Nuggets was one—NBA coaches install set plays as opposed to motion offenses. The 24-second shot clock demands a quick-hitting offense, and the UCLA Series provides it. This play is one you'll see time and again during NBA games, and one we've had tremendous success with at the College of Charleston. Like Option No. 5, it employs a high dribble block. This time, however, the dribble block frees up a mobile small forward to create havoc in the middle of a defense.

Diagrams 4-23 and 4-24: 1, 3 and 5 initiate the offense.

Diagram 4-23.

Diagram 4-24.

Diagram 4-25: After 1 completes his basket cut, he clears to the strongside corner. 4 cuts diagonally to the left block. 2 moves to a right-wing area. 5 steps away from the elbow to set a dribble block for 3.

Diagram 4-26: 3 uses the dribble block to penetrate the defense. Options include a pull-up jump shot, a penetrate-and-kick pass to 2 on the wing, or a pass to 5, rolling to the lane.

Diagram 4-25.

Diagram 4-26.

OPTION NO. 7

Not all teams are blessed with a mobile power forward—a player who can create his own scoring opportunities with quick dribble drives and pull-up shots. Mobile big men with 1-on-1 moves aren't easy to come by these days. But should you have this kind of player on your roster, Option No. 7 promises to isolate him against his opposite number, who may be a step slower, or not effective as a 1-on-1 defender.

Diagrams 4-27 and 4-28: 1, 3 and 5 initiate the offense.

Diagram 4-29: On the flight of the pass from 3 to 5, 1 clears to the strongside corner and 4 screens down, presumably for 2. Instead of using the screen, 2 moves to the left-block area.

Diagram 4-30: 4 flashes back up to the elbow area for a pass from 5. With his teammates and their defenders on the opposite side of the floor, 4 is isolated for 1-on-1 action.

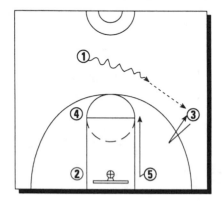

Diagram 4-27.

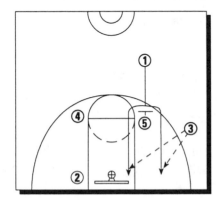

Diagram 4-28.

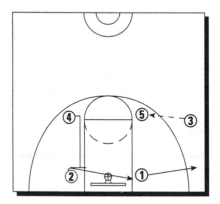

Diagram 4-29.

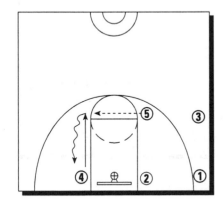

Diagram 4-30.

OPTION NO. 8

In my experience, some of the best 1-on-1 scorers are big guards—players who have a wide range of face-the-basket offensive weapons, including the jump shot, penetrate and pull up move, and slashing moves all the way to the hoop. Like Option No. 7, this play creates an isolation opportunity for the 2 man.

Diagrams 4-31 and 4-32: 1, 3 and 5 initiate the offense. Compared to Option No. 7, 2 and 4 are inverted, with 4 down low and 2 at the elbow area.

Diagram 4-33: On the flight of the pass from 3 to 5, 1 clears to the strongside corner and 2 screens down, presumably for 4. Instead of using the screen, 4 moves to the left-block area.

Diagram 4-34: 2 flashes back up to the elbow area for a pass from 5. With his teammates and their defenders on the opposite side of the floor, 2 is isolated for 1-on-1 action.

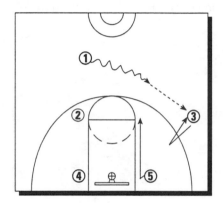

Diagram 4-31.

Diagram 4-32.

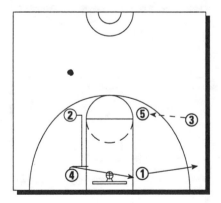

Diagram 4-33.

Diagram 4-34.

OPTION NO. 9

Let's bring the 3 man into the mix. To this point, 3's opportunities have been secondary in nature, or reliant on a dribble block (Option No. 6). In this play, we free up 3 the same way we freed up 4 and 2 with Option Nos. 7 and 8. Much like 2, 3 typically possesses an arsenal of face-the-basket moves. Option No. 9 isolates him against his opposite number, who may be overmatched for size or quickness, or may be in foul trouble.

Diagrams 4-35 and 4-36: To initiate this play, 2 and 3 exchange positions. 1, 2 and 5 initiate the offense.

Diagram 4-37: On the flight of the pass from 2 to 5, 1 clears to the strongside corner and 3 screens down, presumably for 4. Instead of using the screen, 4 moves to the left-block area.

Diagram 4-38: 3 flashes back up to the elbow area for a pass from 5. With his teammates and their defenders on the opposite side of the floor, 3 is isolated for 1-on-1 action.

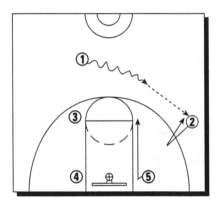

Diagram 4-35.

Diagram 4-36.

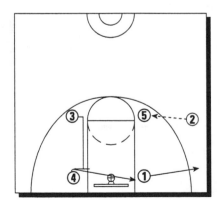

Diagram 4-37.

Diagram 4-38.

OPTION NO. 10

Earlier in this series (Option No. 6), we showed how a high screen (or dribble block) can free up your 3 man for dribble penetration. Why not use the same screening philosophy for a player moving without the ball? Execute well, and you'll get layups. Execute well for a player with excellent athletic ability, and those layups may just be dunks.

Diagram 4-39: Initiate this set play with a pass from 1 to 3, followed by a hand-off from 3 to 1. 4 clears across the lane to the strong side. 2 clears to the top of the key.

Diagram 4-40: 5 steps out from the elbow area to set a screen. 3 uses the screen from 5 to gain an advantage on his defender and move to an open area on the right side of the lane. 1 lobs the ball to 3 for a layup or dunk.

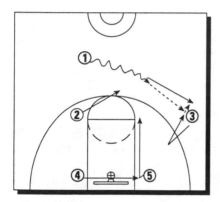

Diagram 4-39.

Diagram 4-40.

OPTION NO. 11

When you think about it, there's really no reason not to lob to 1, even though he may not fit your vision of a slam-dunking finisher. Remember, most of the action leading up to a successful lob play takes place away from the ball. A solid screen, a good pass and catch, and a certain amount of deception all contribute to a successful lob play. Option No. 11 contains all of these elements.

Diagram 4-41: 1, 3 and 5 initiate the play. 4 clears across the lane to the strong side. 2 clears to the top of the key.

Diagram 4-42: To this point, 1 has been limited to two basic moves after his initial pass to 3—using the screen by 5 for a shuffle cut or fade, or following his pass to 3 for a hand-off. Here, 5 sets what figures to be a standard UCLA series screen for a shuffle cut. 1 takes his man to the screen, then loops to an open area on the right side of the lane. 3 lobs to 1 for a layup or dunk.

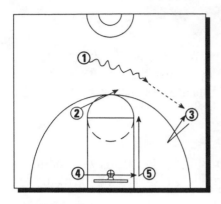

Diagram 4-41.

Diagram 4-42.

OPTION NO. 12

Here's another quick-hitting option for 1, using a dribble block to gain an advantage for a possible drive or pull-up move.

Diagram 4-43: 1, 3 and 5 initiate the offense, with 1 apparently dribbling toward 3 for a standard UCLA Series entry.

Diagram 4-44: 1 reverses to the right side to use a high dribble block set by 4 at the top of the key. 2 clears the floor, creating more space for 1 should he beat his man into the lane.

Diagram 4-45: Should the defense deny 1 the opportunity to penetrate, 4 rolls to the right block for post-up action. If the defense has switched to contain 1, 4 will be covered by 1's original defender, presumably a much smaller player.

Diagram 4-43.

Diagram 4-44.

Diagram 4-45.

OPTION NO. 13

This play produces two options—a quick post-up move for a big man, followed by screen-for-the-screener action, freeing a perimeter player for a jump shot. The first look, for 5 on the block, often surprises the defense, which has grown accustomed to 5 acting primarily as a screener. The second look is a great option for either a two-pointer or a three-pointer, if needed.

Diagram 4-46: Again, the initiation looks like many others in the UCLA Series.

Diagram 4-47: 1 reverses to the right side. 2 moves diagonally up the lane to set what we call a "slide pick" for 5.

Diagram 4-48: Having dribbled to a wing area, 1 can pass to 5, or look for 2 coming off a screen by 4.

Diagram 4-46.

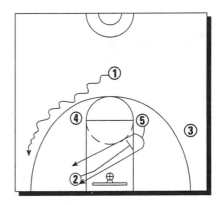

Diagram 4-47.

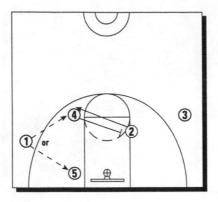

Diagram 4-48.

OPTION NO. 14

One of the most effective ways to free up a scorer for a high-percentage shot is to set staggered screens—two screens set consecutively away from the ball. With this option, we produce a low block opportunity for our center and a foul-line extended jump shot for a guard. With four screens on one play, you may wish to remind your players when practicing this play of the importance of setting big and wide, but legal, screens.

Diagram 4-49: 1 and 5 initiate as usual. 3, instead of cutting back to a wing area, stops at the low left block.

Diagram 4-50: When 1 reverses his dribble, 3 moves up the lane and 2 across the lane to set staggered screens for 5. During practice, remind 2 that he must move out of the lane quickly after setting the screen, or he will be called for a three-second violation.

Diagram 4-49.

Diagram 4-50.

Diagram 4-51: 1 passes to 5 posting up on the low block.

Diagram 4-52: If 5 is overplayed, 2 uses staggered screens by 3 and 4 to free himself up for a jump shot from the right side of the key.

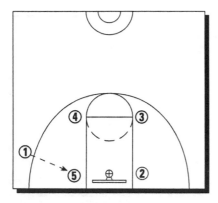

Diagram 4-51.

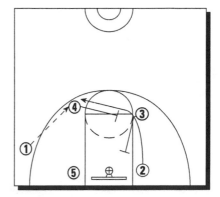

Diagram 4-52.

OPTION NO. 15

Again, setting and using staggered screens is the essence of this play. Instead of 5 and 2 being primary options, this play creates openings for 4 and 3, both coming off staggered screens. With this option, we produce a low block opportunity for a power forward and a foul-line extended jump shot for a small forward.

Diagram 4-53: 1 and 5 initiate as usual. 3, instead of cutting back to a wing area, stops at the low left block.

Diagram 4-54: As 1 continues to the left wing, 2 moves up the lane and 3 across the lane to set staggered screens for 4. During practice, remind 3 that he must move out of the lane quickly after setting the screen, or he will be called for a three-second violation.

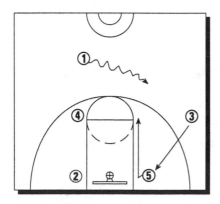

Diagram 4-53.

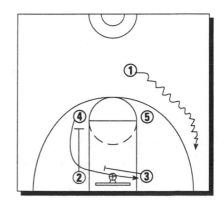

Diagram 4-54.

Diagram 4-55: 1 passes to 4 posting up on the low block.

Diagram 4-56: If 4 is overplayed, 3 uses staggered screens by 2 and 5 to free himself up for a jump shot from the left side of the key.

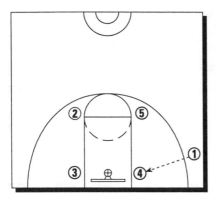

Diagram 4-55.

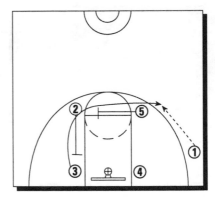

Diagram 4-56.

OPTION NO. 16

If 1 has a hot hand, you may wish to create shooting opportunities for him on the wing. This play gives 1 the option of using staggered screens on one side of the floor or a single screen on the opposite side.

Diagrams 4-57 and 4-58: 1, 3 and 5 initiate the play.

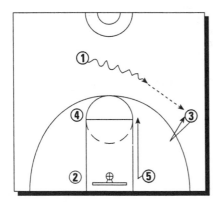

Diagram 4-57.

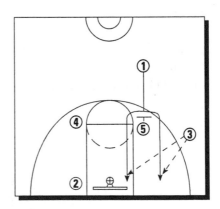

Diagram 4-58.

Diagram 4-59: 3 passes to 5, then moves to the left block. 2 uses a screen by 4 to find an opening at the top of the key.

Diagram 4-60: 1 has the option of using staggered screens by 3 and 5 to pop to an opening on the left wing, or using a single screen by 4 to find an opening on the right wing. 2 makes the pass to 1.

Diagram 4-59.

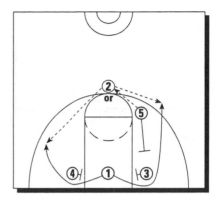

Diagram 4-60.

WHEN YOUR OPPONENT OVERPLAYS THE FIRST PASS

When an opposing coach recognizes your offensive gameplan, he may instruct his players to overplay the initial "entry" pass from 1 to 3. His thought process, which you should anticipate, is that your team can't run the UCLA Series without making that first pass.

Your first response is obvious. Clearly, 3 must be able to free himself from defenders long enough to catch the first pass and face the basket. He must make an aggressive move toward the basket, effectively burying the defender, then explode to the wing position. Even then, however, an aggressive, sticky defender may deny the initial pass from 1 to 3. What then?

We have three options.

Diagram 4-61: Should 3 be overplayed, 1 passes to 5. 5 may then find 3, taking advantage of an overplaying defender, on a backdoor cut to the basket.

Diagram 4-62: Simpler still, 3 makes a backdoor cut and 1 passes to him directly.

Diagram 4-63: 1 and 3 effectively exchange roles. 1 dribbles to the wing area. 3 cuts to the low block setting up where 1 would have been on the first shuffle cut off 5. You can now continue many of the UCLA Series plays we have shown.

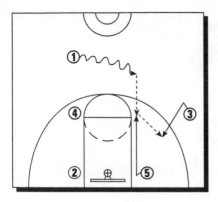

Diagram 4-61.

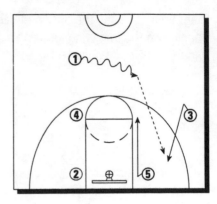

Diagram 4-62.

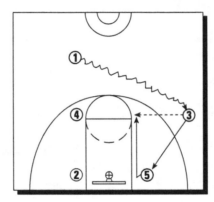

Diagram 4-63.

You can call these variations as play continues or during stoppages, set them up during a timeout, or—if you're fortunate enough to have talented and experienced players—1, 3 and 5 will make adjustments on their own. While these adjustments are particularly useful in high-pressure situations, there also may be some value to using backdoor moves against less aggressive overplays, if only to let your opponent know that you have options. Sometimes, that's enough to discourage a maximum overplay strategy.

DOUBLE YOUR OPTIONS

To this point, we have used 63 diagrams to dissect and present the many and varied options the College of Charleston employs in our version of the UCLA Series. You may have noticed that we presented each option "left-handed"—that is to say, originating on the left side of the floor. This begs the obvious question: Why not run the UCLA Series to the right side? Better yet: Why not run it to both sides?

The answer is: We do! A well-schooled team can run these plays to either side of the floor, effectively doubling its offensive repertoire and adding to the workload of opposing players and coaches. At College of Charleston, we have been blessed over the years with a string of heady, veteran point guards. We occasionally allow our point guard to determine which side of the floor he wants to attack. Whether we as coaches or he as a floor general make this call, the point guard signals the variation by tapping his head, waits for his teammates to adjust the set accordingly, then initiates the play.

CHAPTER 5

More Set Plays: Something for Everyone

In Chapter 4, we detailed a series of 16 plays—the UCLA Series—all originating from a 1-3-1 set. The UCLA Series is superb. It creates all kinds of openings, and gives players a chance to showcase a variety of skills. It is not, however, the be-all and end-all of set-play offense against man-to-man defense. There are times as a coach when I want and need different set-play weapons, whether to isolate a certain player in just the right place on the floor, present different looks and challenges to a defense, milk the clock with a few extra passes, or whatever.

In this chapter, we'll look at 11 set-plays and their variations. When you think about it, between the UCLA Series and its many options and these 11 plays with their options, you are seeing approximately 50 set plays in this book. I know—no coach has the time to install, nor players the time and ability to absorb, the nuances of 50 set plays to attack man-to-man defenses in a half-court setting. Especially not when you consider all of the other strategic challenges you and your team will face during a season.

However, you may see plays in this chapter that fit your team and its personnel perfectly. Go ahead and install them. See whether they work in practice. If all systems are go, call them in a game. You'll be in good company. Many of these plays have been working for a long time at the highest level—the NBA.

These plays originate from a variety of sets. As you recall, the UCLA Series originates from a 1-3-1 set. These plays originate from many formations, including the 1-3-1, 1-2-2, 2-1-2, Double Stack and Single Stack sets. For the purpose of this book, we have organized and presented them by their original set.

THE 1-3-1 SET: ATLANTA

When I was an assistant to Lou Carnesecca at St. John's University, I attended a clinic conducted by Hubie Brown, the television basketball analyst who was then head coach of the NBA's Atlanta Hawks. Coach Brown showed me a play that generated three separate looks for a power forward, 4. In recognition of the play's origin, we call it Atlanta.

Atlanta
Diagram 5-1: Atlanta originates in a 1-3-1 set. 1 dribbles right and passes to 4 on the wing. 1 loops behind 4 on the wing and takes a handoff or short pass from his teammate.

Diagram 5-2: 4 fakes a clearing move to the opposite side, turns and posts up on the low block. At the same time, 5 screens diagonally down the lane for 3 to flash to the elbow area.

Diagram 5-3: 1's first look is to 4 on the low block.

Diagram 5-4: If 4 is overplayed from the baseline side, 1 passes to 3, who looks for 4. 2 pops out to the opposite wing area.

Diagram 5-1.

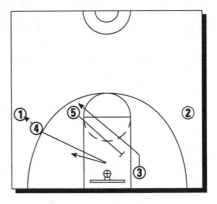

Diagram 5-2.

Diagram 5-3.

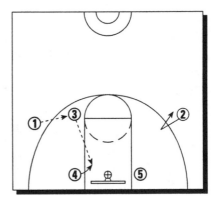

Diagram 5-4.

Diagram 5-5: Should 3 pass crosscourt to 2, 5 sets a screen across the lane for 4. 4 can go either way, baseline or over the screen, to free himself up on the low block.

Diagram 5-6: 2 passes to 4.

Diagram 5-5.

Diagram 5-6.

THE 1-2-2 SET: INDIANA, POP OUT AND MIDDLE

These three plays originate from a 1-2-2 half-court set. See Diagram 5-7.

Indiana

Younger coaches may not remember just how good a team the Indiana Pacers were during their days in the American Basketball Association. The Pacers were a perennial championship contender. They featured some great players—George McGinness, Roger Brown and Mel Daniels, among others—and Coach Bob "Slick" Leonard knew how to get those players free for high-percentage scoring opportunities. During my days as an assistant coach of the ABA's New York Nets, I saw this play many times. At College of Charleston, it became a cornerstone of our set-play offense.

Diagram 5-8: 1 initiates the offense by dribbling left, then reversing to the right. This action forces the defense to adjust and creates better passing lanes. On the dribble reversal, 2 screens down from the foul line-extended area for 3, then clears through to the opposite side.

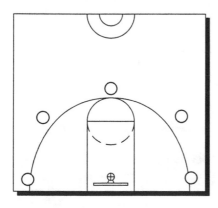

Diagram 5-7.

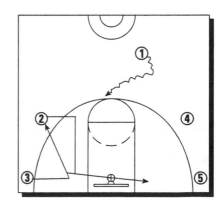

Diagram 5-8.

Diagram 5-9: On reaching the top of the key, 1 passes to 3, then moves to the opposite foul line-extended area to set a screen for 4. 4 can go either way off the screen, depending on how his defender is playing him. 3 passes to 4 for a lay-up or short jump shot. After setting the screen, 1 pops back to the top of the key. 5 steps in toward the low block for rebounding position.

Diagram 5-10: Should 3 be unable to pass to 4, he passes to 1. On the flight of the pass, 5 screens for 2, who pops out to a wing area.

Diagram 5-9.

Diagram 5-10.

Diagram 5-11: 1 passes to 2, who looks for 5 posting up after his screen for 2. On the opposite side of the floor, 3 screens for 4 moving to the wing.

Diagram 5-12: 1 may pass to 4, who looks for 3 on a quick post-up move.

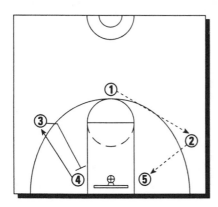

Diagram 5-11.

Diagram 5-12.

Pop Out

This play is a quick hitter for 3. However, be aware that you can run it to either side of the floor or to a different player, should his post-up skills warrant that look.

Diagram 5-13: When 1 reverses his dribble, 3 screens for 2 popping out to the wing. 4 and 5 exchange to occupy defenders of the opposite side of the floor.

Diagram 5-14: 1 passes to 2, who finds 3 spinning back from his screen for a quick post-up move.

Diagram 5-13.

Diagram 5-14.

Middle

Middle offers a variety of opportunities for inside players using screens. It may be run to either side of the floor.

Diagram 5-15: 1 uses a change-of-direction dribble to free himself at the top of the key. 2 and 3 pop out to wing areas of opposite sides of the floor.

Diagram 5-16: 1 opts to pass to 2 on the right wing. After passing, 1 sets a screen near the left elbow for 3. 2 passes to 3 for a high-percentage interior opportunity. After his screen, 1 returns to the top of the key as an outlet.

Diagram 5-17: Should 3 be covered or overplayed, 2 passes back to 1. 3 sets a screen near the low right block for 4, then clears to the corner. 4 uses 3's screen to free himself up for a pass from 1.

Diagram 5-18: If 1 can not find 4, he passes back to 2 on the right wing. 4 screens for 5, flashing into the lane. 2 passes to 5.

Diagram 5-15.

Diagram 5-16.

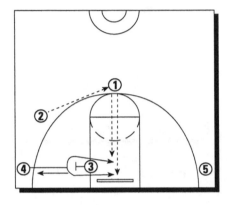

Diagram 5-17.

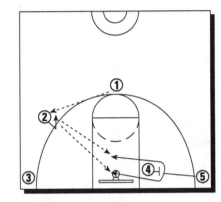

Diagram 5-18.

Diagram 5-19: 1 initiates the offense to the left side of the floor with a pass to 3. 1 sets a screen for 2. 3 passes to 2 in the lane.

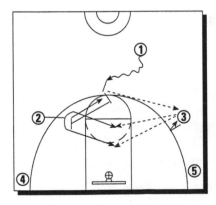

Diagram 5-19.

Diagrams 5-20 and 5-21: These show the continuation of Middle when initiated to the left side of the floor. 2 screens for 5. 5 screens for 4.

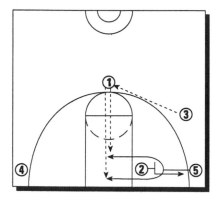

Diagram 5-20.

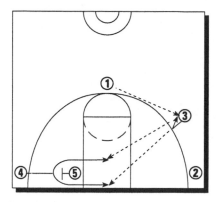

Diagram 5-21.

THE 2-1-2 AND 2-3 SETS: GREENVILLE AND RUSSELL

These plays originate from similar sets. Greenville originates from a 2-1-2 set. See Diagram 5-22. Russell originates from a 2-3 set. See Diagram 5-23.

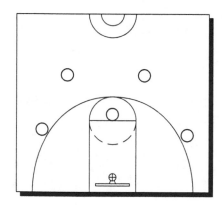

Diagram 5-22.

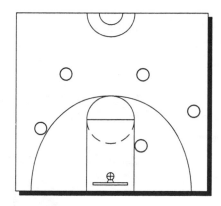

Diagram 5-23.

Greenville

In my early years at College of Charleston, one of our great rivals was Presbyterian College, coached by Butch Estes. Coach Estes moved on to Furman University, located in Greenville, SC, where his teams used this play to great effect. No wonder—Greenville creates many scoring opportunities. Initially, it frees a guard on a cut to the basket. Later, a forward uses a backpick for a quick flash and post-up opportunity. A third option, staggered screens for a guard, often creates an open jump shot.

Greenville may be run to either side of the floor, as we'll show you here.

Diagram 5-24: 1 initiates the offense on the right side of the floor. 3 pops to a wing area for a pass from 1. On the pass from 1 to 3, 5 screens for 2, who makes a UCLA-type shuffle cut to the basket. 3 passes to 2 for a layup or pull-up shot.

Diagram 5-25: If 2 is not open for the initial pass, 3 passes to 1, then uses a backpick by 2 to post up on the left side. 1 passes to 5, who passes to 4. 4 looks inside to 3.

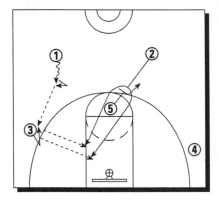

Diagram 5-24.

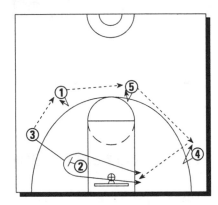

Diagram 5-25.

Diagram 5-26: If 3 is not open, 1 and 5 set staggered screens for 2. Note, this is not a double screen, but rather two separate screens used by the same cutter, 2. 4 passes to 2.

Diagram 5-27: To initiate the play to the left side, 1 passes across the top of the key to 2.

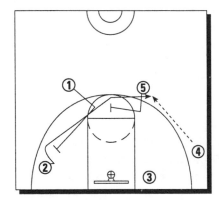

Diagram 5-26.

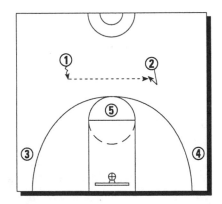

Diagram 5-27.

Diagram 5-28: 2 passes to 4 on the left wing. On the flight of the pass from 2 to 4, 1 shuffle cuts off of 5's screen. 4 passes to 1 for a layup or pull-up shot.

Diagram 5-29: Should 1 be covered on the initial cut, he sets a backpick. 4 passes to 2, then uses 1's backpick for a quick cut and post-up move on the opposite block. 2 passes to 5, who passes to 3. 3 looks inside for 4.

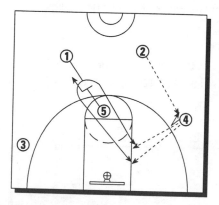

Diagram 5-28.

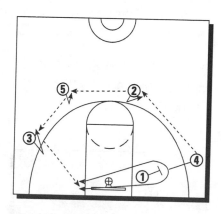

Diagram 5-29.

Diagram 5-30: This time, 1 uses staggered screens by 2 and 5 to free himself up for a pass from 3.

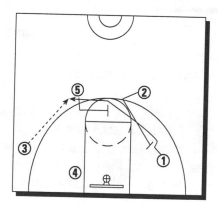

Diagram 5-30.

Russell

When I was an assistant at St. John's University, we were blessed with many talented athletes and scorers. This play is named after the forward David Russell, who finished it with regularity and flair during his career at St. John's.

Like many of our set plays, Russell may be run to either side of the floor. It differs in the sense that changing sides is a definite "call"—not an option. When we run Russell, we call either Russell Right or Russell Left before setting up and initiating the play.

Diagram 5-31: Here's Russell Right. 1 initiates the offense by dribbling to the right side of the key, then passing across the top of the key to 2. After the pass, 1 replaces 3 in the right-wing area. 3 cuts to the basket without the ball. 4 fakes toward 2. 5 steps out from the low block area.

Diagram 5-32: 2 skips the ball to 1. 4 uses a backpick by 5 and a screen across the lane by 3 to free himself up on the low right block. 1 passes to 4 or 3, who rolls to the right-elbow area.

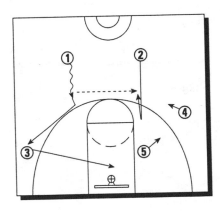

Diagram 5-31.

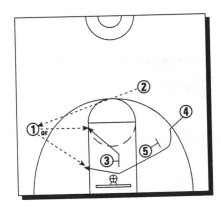

Diagram 5-32.

Diagram 5-33: 5 sets a screen for 2, who fades to the wing area as a skip pass or option from 1.

Diagrams 5-34, 5-35 and 5-36: Here's Russell Left. In this variation, we typically ask our 1, 2 and 5 players to fill the same roles. 3 and 4 exchange roles. 3 uses two screens for a post-up move. 4 screens, then rolls to an elbow area. As a game progresses, a coach must evaluate match-ups on an ongoing basis, and use his players in the most advantageous way.

Diagram 5-33.

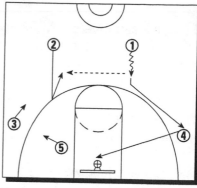

Diagram 5-34.

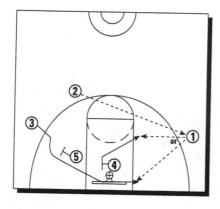

Diagram 5-35.

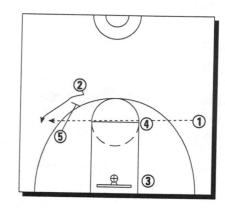

Diagram 5-36.

THE DOUBLE STACK: TEXAS

At the College of Charleston, we run one set play, Texas, from the Double Stack set. The term "double stack" is very descriptive. In our double stack set, we typically stack a post player and a wing player on both sides of the lane. See Diagram 5-37.

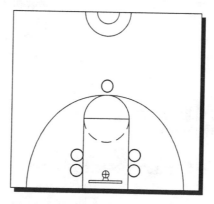

Diagram 5-37.

Texas

During our early years of NCAA Division I scheduling, we played a home-and-home series against Texas-Arlington. I remember three things most clearly about those games. First, Texas-Arlington was a very talented team—Lakers general manager Jerry West scouted one of their players during our game at Arlington. Second, Texas-Arlington played its home games on stage in a theater, with tip-off preceded by a fireworks display—a most unusual scenario. And third, Texas-Arlington ran an intriguing and effective continuity offense against man-to-man defenses.

The following year, we refined and installed Texas as one of our offensive options. I present it as a set play, because it is so patterned and creates immediate opportunities. Another benefit to Texas: You may enter it from either side of the floor.

Diagram 5-38: 1 initiates the offense by dribbling to the top of the key. 2 and 3 pop out to wing areas as potential pass receivers.

Diagram 5-39: 1 initiates a left-side entry by passing to 3, who looks immediately to 5 posting up. After his initial pass, 1 screens for 4, flashing up the lane to the key area.

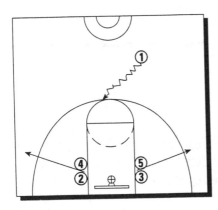

Diagram 5-38.

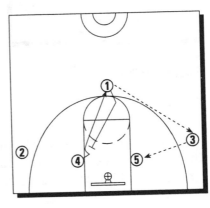

Diagram 5-39.

Diagram 5-40: Should 5 be overplayed, 3 passes to 4, who may have a better angle for a quick pass inside to 5. 1 loops out of the lane to the right wing. 2 cuts toward the low left block.

Diagram 5-41: 4 passes to 1, then screens down for 2. 2 screens for 5, cutting across the lane, then pops out to the top of the key.

Diagram 5-42: 1 passes to 5 for a shot, or to 2, who may have an open shot or a better angle for a pass to 5.

Diagram 5-43: Should 2 pass to 3, he then sets a screen for 5 coming up the lane. 3 looks for 4 on a post-up move.

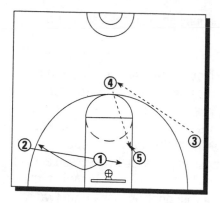

Diagram 5-40.

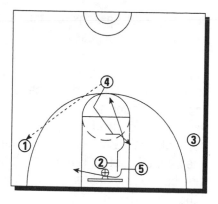

Diagram 5-41.

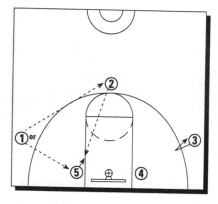

Diagram 5-42.

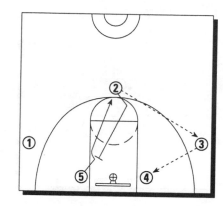

Diagram 5-43.

Diagram 5-44: Should 4 be overplayed, 3 passes to 5 to create a better angle for the pass inside. 2 loops out of the lane to the right wing. 1 cuts toward the low left block.

Diagram 5-45: 5 passes to 2, then screens down for 1. 1 screens for 4, cutting across the lane, then pops out to the top of the key.

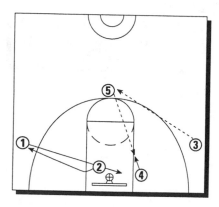

Diagram 5-44.

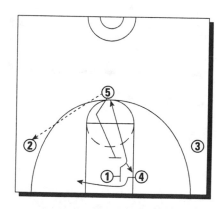

Diagram 5-45.

Diagram 5-46: 2 passes to 4 for a shot, or to 1, who may have an open shot or a better angle for a pass to 4.

Diagrams 5-47 through 5-55: 1 may choose or you may instruct him to initiate the offense to the right side. In that event, 1 passes to 2 to enter the offense. From there, the action essentially mirrors what took place with a left-side entry. In our experience, quick openings are available in Texas. Its beauty, however, is that you can make as many passes as you need to create an opportunity. If the initial, unscreened post-up is not available, the second post-up, created by a screen across may be. In either instance, the post player gets two looks—one from the wing, the other from the top of the key. This way, you double your post-up looks from two to four, all within four passes.

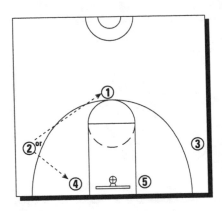

Diagram 5-46.

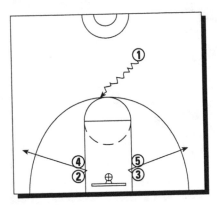

Diagram 5-47.

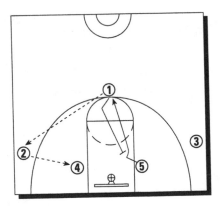

Diagram 5-48.

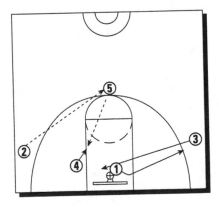

Diagram 5-49.

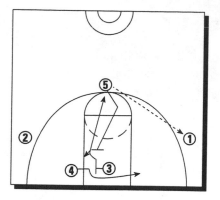

Diagram 5-50.

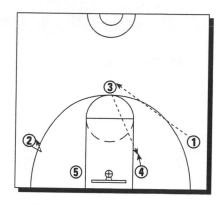

Diagram 5-51.

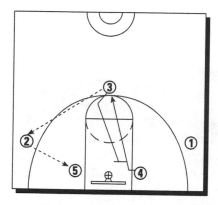

Diagram 5-52.

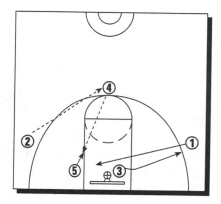

Diagram 5-53.

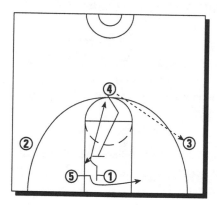

Diagram 5-54.

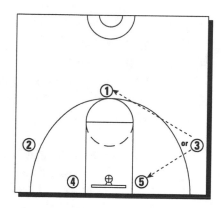

Diagram 5-55.

THE SINGLE STACK LEFT: CALIFORNIA AND KANSAS

In a Single Stack Left set, we stack 3 and 5 on the left block, with 4 on the opposite block and 2 on the opposite wing. See Diagram 5-56. This puts our players in ideal position to initiate two potent set plays, California and Kansas.

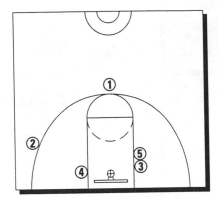

Diagram 5-56.

California

Former University of California coach Pete Newell is one of the legends of the game. His Golden Bears were championship-caliber teams. To this day, Coach Newell is a highly regarded clinician and consultant on big men. Many NBA and college-level centers fine-tune their post games with the help of Coach Newell.

Like Texas, California is a continuity offense. Given Coach Newell's affinity for big men, it's no surprise that this offense creates great post-up opportunities for forwards—5, 4 and 3.

Another coach who has used this offense to great effect is Bob Knight. During his tenure at Army, Coach Knight's teams engaged in some memorable nailbiters with St. John's. A big part of an undermanned Army team's success was its ability to give its players an edge through this offense.

Diagram 5-57: 1 initiates the offense by dribbling to the top of the key. 3 pops out of the stack to a wing area. 1 passes to 3, then loops around 3 to the corner. 2 replaces 1 at the top of the key. 4 replaces 2 on the right wing.

Diagram 5-58: 3 looks immediately to 5 posting up.

Diagram 5-59: If 5 is not open, 3 passes to 2 at the top of the key. 5 steps off the block. 4 frees himself up on the wing.

Diagram 5-60: 2 passes to 4. 5 screens for 3, then rolls to the left-elbow area. 3 uses 5's screen to free himself up on the right block.

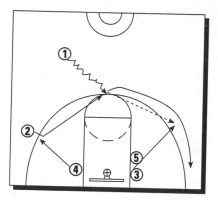

Diagram 5-57.

Diagram 5-58.

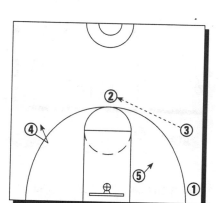

Diagram 5-59.

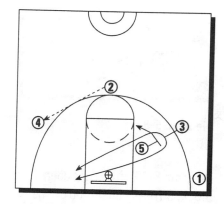

Diagram 5-60.

Diagram 5-61: 4 looks for 3 on a post-up move or 5 at the opposite elbow. 2 loops around 4 to the right corner. 1 replaces 2 at the top of the key. If 5 does not receive a pass, he steps out to a wing area.

Diagram 5-62: If 3 is not open, 4 passes to 1 at the top of the key. 3 steps off the block. 5 frees himself up on the wing.

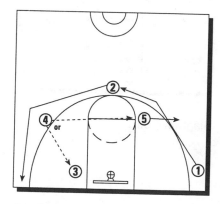

Diagram 5-61.

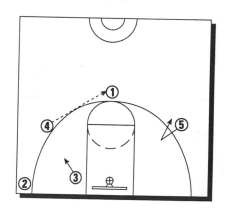

Diagram 5-62.

Diagram 5-63: 1 passes to 5. 3 screens for 4, then rolls to the right-elbow area. 4 uses 3's screen to free himself up on the left block.

Diagram 5-64: 5 looks for 4 on a post-up move or 3 at the opposite elbow. 1 loops around 5 to the left corner. 2 replaces 1 at the top of the key. If 3 does not receive a pass, he steps out to a wing area.

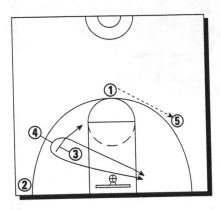

Diagram 5-63.

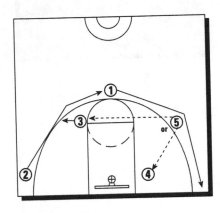

Diagram 5-64.

Diagram 5-65: If 4 is not open, 5 passes to 2 at the top of the key. 4 steps off the block. 3 frees himself up on the wing.

Diagram 5-66: 2 passes to 3. 4 screens for 5, then rolls to the left-elbow area. 5 uses 4's screen to free himself up on the right block.

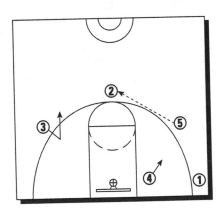

Diagram 5-65.

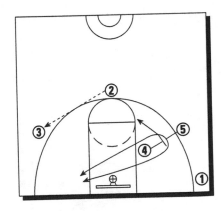

Diagram 5-66.

Diagram 5-67: 3 looks for 5 on a post-up move or 4 at the opposite elbow.

Diagram 5-68: At some point, whether because your team isn't moving as well as it should, or your opponent is overplaying on the perimeter, your wing players may find that the pass to the top of the key is not open. Here are two options. In the first, 3 passes to 1, then uses 5's screen for a give-and-go scoring cut. 1 passes to 3 for a layup or pull-up shot.

Diagram 5-69: 4 recognizes the overplay and sets a screen for 2. 2 backdoor cuts to the basket for a pass from 3.

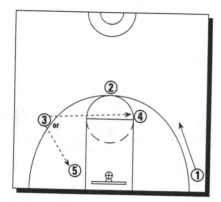

Diagram 5-67.

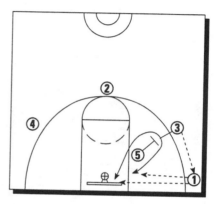

Diagram 5-68.

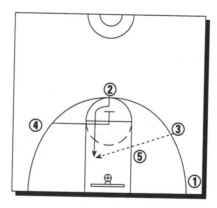

Diagram 5-69.

Kansas

Kansas is a quick hitter that creates post-up action for 5, a flash for 4, and a skip pass to a perimeter shooter 1.

Diagram 5-70: 1 initiates the offense by dribbling to the top of the key. 3 pops out to a wing area. 1 passes to 3.

Diagram 5-71: On the flight of the pass from 1 to 3, 5 posts up and 4 flashes to the ballside elbow. Away from the ball, 2 backpicks for 1, who loops to a wing area. 3 passes to 5 or 4, who may also look inside for 5.

Diagram 5-72: Should 5 and 4 be covered, 1 is an excellent option for a pass from 3.

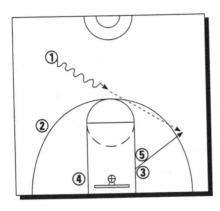

Diagram 5-70.

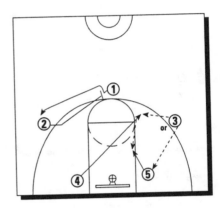

Diagram 5-71.

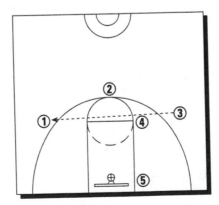

Diagram 5-72.

THE SINGLE STACK RIGHT: JACKSONVILLE

In setting up the Single Stack Right formation used in Jacksonville, we generally put a post and a 2-guard in the stack and the "finisher" at the foul-line area. The finisher is always a forward or center. This enables us to use 1 as the initiator, 2 as a passer, a big man screening and a forward scoring on a quick post-up move. See Diagram 5-73.

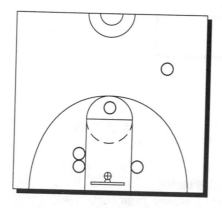

Diagram 5-73.

Jacksonville

Over the years, Jacksonville University has entrusted its basketball program to some excellent coaching minds—Bob Wenzel and Rich Haddad among them. Both trace their coaching roots to South Carolina; Wenzel as an assistant at South Carolina and Haddad as one of my assistants at College of Charleston. When Wenzel left Jacksonville for Rutgers, Haddad succeeded him. One set play that worked very well for both of them (and us) is Jacksonville.

In this section, we will show all of Jacksonville's variations—left and right, for the 5, 4 and 3 men. All six variations have two things in common. First, off-the-ball player movement begins when 1 dribbles across the imaginary line bisecting the court lengthwise. Second, within two passes, your finisher will have a high-percentage scoring opportunity.

Diagram 5-74: Here is the left-to-right initiation of Jacksonville with 5 as the primary finisher. 1 dribbles up the left side of the court, then turns right across the top of the key. 2 pops out to a low-wing area.

Diagram 5-75: When 1 crosses the top of the key, 3 and 5 exchange. 1 passes to 2. On the flight of the pass, 4 sets a screen across the lane for 5 and spins back to the ballside elbow area. 5 cuts to the ballside block on the baseline side of 4's screen. 3 returns to the low left block for rebounding position.

Diagram 5-74.

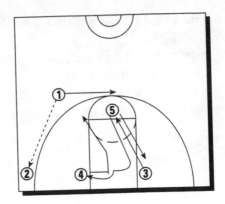

Diagram 5-75.

Diagram 5-76: 2 passes to 5 or 4 for a scoring opportunity.

Diagram 5-77: Here is the right-to-left initiation of Jacksonville with 5 as the primary finisher. 1 dribbles up the right side of the court, then turns left across the top of the key. 2 runs the baseline from right to left, popping out to a low-wing area.

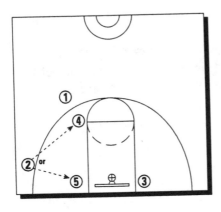

Diagram 5-76.

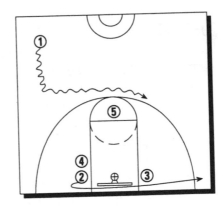

Diagram 5-77.

Diagram 5-78: When 1 crosses the top of the key, 4 and 5 exchange. 1 passes to 2. On the flight of the pass, 3 sets a screen across the lane for 5 and spins back to the ballside elbow area. 5 cuts to the ballside block on the baseline side of 3's screen. 4 returns to the low right block for rebounding position.

Diagram 5-79: 2 passes to 5 or 3 for a scoring opportunity.

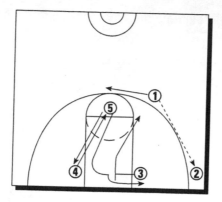

Diagram 5-78.

Diagram 5-79.

Diagrams 5-80 through 5-82: Here is the left-to-right initiation of Jacksonville for 4.

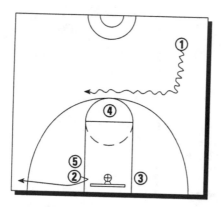

Diagram 5-80.

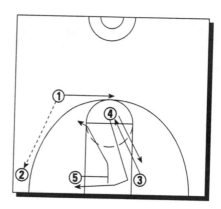

Diagram 5-81.

Diagram 5-82.

Diagrams 5-83 through 5-85: Here is the right-to-left initiation of Jacksonville for 4.

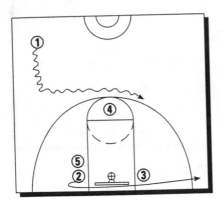

Diagram 5-83.

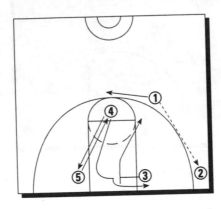

Diagram 5-84.

Diagram 5-85.

Diagrams 5-86 through 5-88: Here is the left-to-right initiation of Jacksonville for 3.

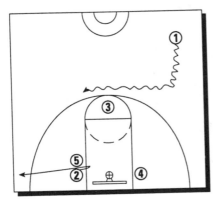

Diagram 5-86.

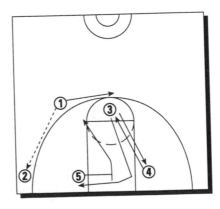

Diagram 5-87.

Diagram 5-88.

Diagrams 5-89 through 5-91: Here is the right-to-left initiation of Jacksonville for 3.

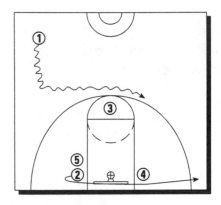

Diagram 5-89.

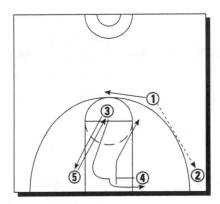

Diagram 5-90.

Diagram 5-91.

UNIQUE SETS: DOUBLE AND TURNOVER

Two of our set plays originate from sets that defy simple classification. These plays create excellent scoring opportunities, and should be considered for inclusion in your arsenal of set plays.

Double

Double is so named because it employs a double screen to create attractive, high-percentage options. Double's three options produce advantageous post-up positioning for 3 and 4, and jump shots for 3 and 2.

Diagram 5-92: 1 initiates the action by dribbling from left to right across the top of the key. 2 sets a screen across the lane for 3, then loops around a double screen by 4 and 5.

Diagram 5-93: 1 passes to 3 posting up or 2 for a jump shot. 4 and 5 move to the weak side of the floor for rebounding position.

Note: One key element of Double is legal screening by 2, 4 and 5. Beyond setting legal screens, 4 and 5 must clear from the lane promptly or risk being called for a three-second violation.

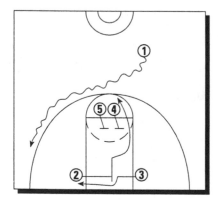

Diagram 5-92.

Diagram 5-93.

Diagram 5-94: The second option off of Double begins with 3 using the double screen by 4 and 5. 2 clears across the lane.

Diagram 5-95: 5 screens for 4, who loops to the low block on the block. 1 passes to 4 posting up or 3 for a jump shot.

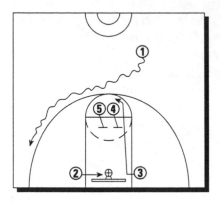

Diagram 5-94.

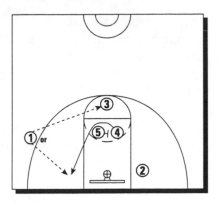

Diagram 5-95.

Diagram 5-96: The third option off Double begins with 3 looping around the double screen by 4 and 5 to establish position on the ballside low block. Instead of clearing across the lane, 2 follows 3 around the double screen to an opening above the foul line.

Diagram 5-97: 1 passes to 3 posting up or 2 for a jump shot.

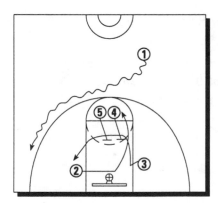

Diagram 5-96.

Diagram 5-97.

Turnover

Turnover creates a specific scoring opportunity or opportunities for every player on the floor. It may be run to either side of the floor, but only when called, not as an option. For example, when calling the play, you would specify Turnover Right or Turnover Left, if you have both in your playbook.

Diagram 5-98: Here is Turnover, initiated from right to left. 1 initiates the play by dribbling up the right side of the floor, then to his left across the top of the key. 5 steps out from the foul line to set a high dribble block for 1. 2 begins to loop to the opposite side of the floor, using a screen by 3. Should 1 gain a quick advantage off the high dribble block, he is free to penetrate or pull up for a shot or pass.

Diagram 5-99: If 1 does not gain a significant advantage, he continues dribbling to a left-wing area. 2 completes his cut to the left corner, using screens by 3 and 4.

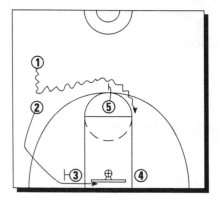

Diagram 5-98.

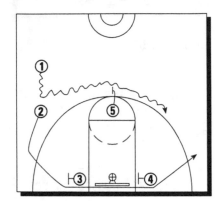

Diagram 5-99.

Diagram 5-100: 1 passes to 2, who may be open for a jump shot or a quick look inside to 4 posting up on the low block. On the other side of the floor, 3 screens for 5, then steps to the top of the key as an outlet. 5 uses 3's screen for a cut to the basket.

Diagram 5-101: Should 2 be overplayed defensively or if 5 is wide open, 1 passes to 5 for a layup or short jump shot.

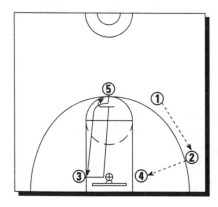

Diagram 5-100.

Diagram 5-101.

Diagram 5-102: It's possible that an alert, well-schooled defense will take away 1's looks to both 2 and 5. Should this occur, 1 passes to 3. 3 may pass directly to 5 coming back up the lane or may dribble to a wing area to improve his angle for a post entry pass to 5.

Diagram 5-103: Here's another option. 3 screens up the lane for 5, then steps out to the top of the key. 1 looks to 5.

Diagram 5-102.

Diagram 5-103.

Diagram 5-104: If not open, 5 clears through the lane. 1 passes to 3 for 1-on-1, dribble-penetration action.

Diagrams 5-105 through 5-111: Here is Turnover initiated from left to right.

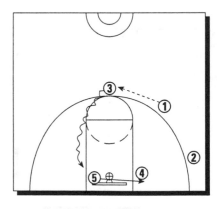

Diagram 5-104.

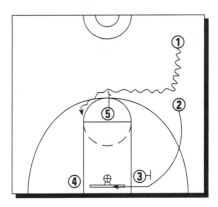

Diagram 5-105.

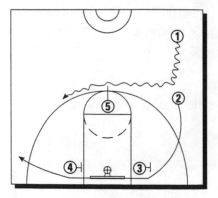

Diagram 5-106.

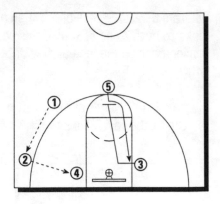

Diagram 5-107.

Diagram 5-108.

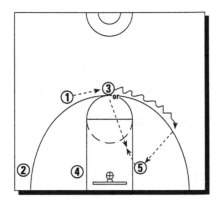

Diagram 5-109.

Diagram 5-110.

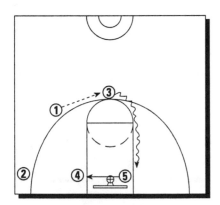

Diagram 5-111.

CHAPTER 6

Breakdown Offense: Flex Plus

Chapters 4 and 5 presented dozens of set plays for attacking man-to-man defenses in a half-court setting. In a perfect world, your team would execute its set plays so well that they would always result in a high-percentage shot. The reality is, nobody's perfect. In the heat of battle, players occasionally fail to execute. Physical and mental miscues happen; they're part of the game. And that's just your team. What if your opponents, through great scouting, strong play or both, simply shut down a play?

WHAT THEN?

At College of Charleston, the answer is: breakdown offense. To be successful at any level of competition, your team must be able to run at least one patterned, well-conceived breakdown system. What do I mean by breakdown offense? Unlike set plays, which are designed to produce one or two specific, high-percentage opportunities, a breakdown offense creates opportunities for all five players on the floor. Instead of specific, prescribed ball and player movement, a breakdown offense establishes and operates within a set of guidelines, promoting ball and player movement within those guidelines. Unlike a set play, a breakdown offense is a "continuity," which may be run for as many passes as needed to generate a high-percentage shot, within the constraints of a shot clock.

In Chapters 6 and 7, we present two breakdown offenses—Flex Plus and Motion—suggesting general guidelines for their use and execution, and diagramming options within each system. Depending on your experience in the game, you'll recognize elements of each offense. I strongly encourage you to build at least one of these systems into your team's offensive gameplan. We use two, because each presents its own unique wrinkles and options. Depending on personnel and other considerations, you may install one, both or neither. Whatever your decision, understand that no man-to-man offensive system is complete without a breakdown option.

In theory, you may install either Flex Plus or Motion as your exclusive man-to-man offense. These systems are basic, sound and proven effective at all levels, from elementary school to the National Basketball Association. Anyone who watched the 1997 NBA Finals will recognize elements of these offenses in the system employed by the Utah Jazz. Years earlier, the Denver Nuggets under Coach Doug Moe employed many of these breakdown principles on a full-time basis instead of running traditional set plays.

WHERE AND WHEN

We always call a set play after our opponent makes a field goal or makes or misses a foul shot. After a missed field goal or turnover, if we don't have a fast break opportunity, we call a set play. We also call set plays after violations and timeouts, particularly when inbounding in the backcourt.

So, when do breakdown offenses come into play?

We break down to our Motion offense at the end of fast break and secondary break opportunities, or if a front-court inbounding play doesn't work. We also run Flex Plus or Motion when a set play breaks down—if our opponent stops a pass that would continue a play or forces our dribbler away from the next pass. Our players recognize these situations and reset into a breakdown offense.

Getting into a breakdown offense is a matter of recognition and organization. In most instances, we break down into Flex Plus or Motion "on the fly"—without a stoppage in play. Our players know, from pre-game scouting and coaching during the game, which breakdown offense we wish to employ in a given situation. Once a breakdown situation occurs, the player with the ball recognizes it and calls for a specific breakdown offense. The players then organize themselves in appropriate perimeter and interior positions.

Breakdown offenses can be used to milk the clock, patiently attacking the basket without getting into an all-out delay game. The ability to work the clock in this fashion may be more valuable now that rulesmakers have re-installed the five-second, closely-guarded rule. For several years, coaches simply put the ball in their point guard's hands and let him pound it near midcourt, killing precious seconds. The closely-guarded rule will negate some, if not all, of that kind of action.

FLEX PLUS

Any student of the game recognizes the Flex offense. Many college and high school teams employ the Flex, or some of its principles, to generate high-percentage scoring opportunities. The Flex is an excellent offense if you like a system that combines continuity with clear-cut rules. Passing, screening and use of screens are fundamental building blocks of traditional Flex-style offense. When a Flex offense is clicking on all cylinders, you rarely see a dribble.

We call our version of this offense Flex Plus because it enhances the traditional, step-by-step Flex offense with attractive inside and outside options. Over the years, we've found that this flexibility is a major plus. We've also found that Flex Plus is a real conversation piece in clinics and chalk talks. Other coaches love it; many use it.

In Flex Plus, we keep our center (5) around the basket for scoring, screening and rebounding. The center moves from block to block, using or setting screens, and posting up when the opportunity presents itself. This represents a significant variation from the center's role in the traditional Flex offense. In the Flex, the center often moves off the block for jump shots and other face-the-basket action. Even with this wrinkle, Flex Plus generates backpick-postup action and an attractive array of perimeter opportunities from the key, wings and corners.

Flex Plus is particularly useful if your center is immobile or lacks passing and perimeter shooting skills. Flex Plus positions this kind of center to do what he does best—screen, use screens and post up.

Meanwhile, on the perimeter, players' options in Flex Plus include elbow-to-elbow and elbow-to-corner passing, elbow-to-elbow dribbling, an occasional pick on the ball, and a pass-and-go-behind move. This variety of options is significantly wider than seen in the regular Flex offense. While the Flex promotes elbow-to-elbow passing and subsequent action, it limits elbow-to-corner passing, discourages elbow-to-elbow dribbling, and rarely employs picks on the ball or the kind of hand-off action you'll see later in this chapter.

What skills will your perimeter players need to make Flex Plus work?

Ideally, your personnel will include a center and four mobile players, who fill perimeter positions 15 to 18 feet from each other. This spacing maximizes opportunities generated by ball and player movement. Once stationed appropriately on the floor, your four perimeter players should be able to pass, cut, screen and, of course, knock down the open jump shot, whether a two-pointer or a three.

It's important that your perimeter players take every opportunity to look inside. This not only keeps the defense honest by presenting an interior threat; it also keeps your big man happy. In my experience, a happy big man on the offensive end is a more productive big man on the defensive end, where the center's post defense, rebounding and shot-blocking skills are critical elements in your team's success.

BASIC GUIDELINES FOR FLEX PLUS

Aside from when to use it, personnel considerations, and spacing, the basic guidelines of Flex Plus offense involve ball and player movement. When the ball is passed from one spot on the floor to another, prescribed cuts and screens occur. Within these movements are options and wrinkles that make Flex Plus what it is—a Flex-style offense that is less predictable than the traditional Flex.

Five basic guidelines govern the College of Charleston's Flex Plus offense. These are:

- Cuts and screens following an elbow-to-corner pass;
- Cuts and screens following an elbow-to-elbow pass;
- Screening across the lane;
- Downscreen-and-fade action; and
- Postup and "hold" action.

In the following diagrams, we'll illustrate these guidelines, including their variations.

DIAGRAMS OF FLEX PLUS ACTION

Diagram 6-1: Here's a typical elbow-to-corner pass, with the center (5) opposite the ball. Following the pass to the corner, the passer cuts to the basket for give-and-go or post-up action. If neither is there, the cutter screens across the lane for 5, who posts up on the ball side. Once the passer cuts to the basket, other perimeter players rotate to fill spots as outlets. (We illustrate perimeter rotation in subsequent diagrams, 6-12 through 6-15.)

Diagram 6-2: What happens when the center is on the same side as the ball? The rule is simple: we never cut to an occupied post. Instead of cutting to the basket after his elbow-to-corner pass, the passer clears to the opposite corner. 5 posts up.

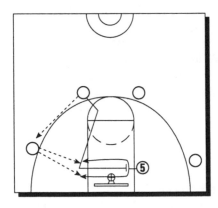

Diagram 6-1.

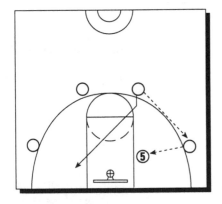

Diagram 6-2.

Diagram 6-3: On an elbow-to-elbow pass, we look to pass and screen down. In this case, the pass is made from the elbow opposite the center. After passing to the left elbow, the passer screens down for his teammate in the corner, who looks for a quick pass and jump shot in the right elbow area. The original passer replaces his teammate in the corner.

Diagram 6-4: Same situation; different finish. Instead of using the downscreen to create a jump shot opportunity, the player coming out of the corner cuts backdoor or curls over the top of the screen. This can catch a guessing or overplaying defender out of position. Again, the screener replaces his teammate in the corner.

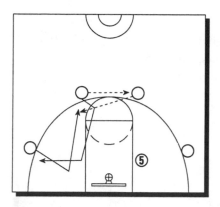

Diagram 6-3.

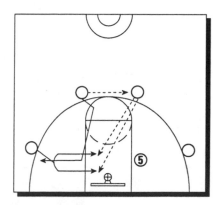

Diagram 6-4.

Diagram 6-5: Here's a logical continuation of movement illustrated in Diagram 6-4. After executing a backdoor or curl move, the player continues across the lane and screens for 5, who posts up on the right side. The player with the ball at the elbow may skip pass to the original downscreener who faded to the corner, feed 5 directly, or dribble to the right elbow to improve his angle for a pass to 5.

Diagram 6-6: This time, the elbow-to-elbow pass originates on the same side as the center (5). The passer screens down for his teammate coming out of the corner for a jump-shot opportunity.

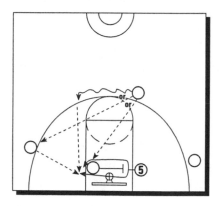

Diagram 6-5.

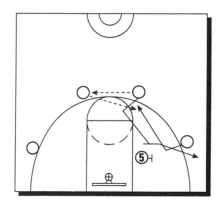

Diagram 6-6.

Diagram 6-7: Again, the elbow-to-elbow pass originates on the same side as the center. The passer downscreens, then clears to the corner. The player coming out of the corner uses a backpick by 5 to backdoor or curl to an opening. The first option is a pass to the player coming across the lane. The second option is a skip pass to the downscreener, who has faded off a screen by 5 to the corner. This opens up a jump shot or pass to 5 posting up.

Diagram 6-8: You never know just how your opponents will react to your Flex Plus attack. Should they aggressively deny potential passing outlets, a player can come out of the corner and set a dribble block, freeing the dribbler for a quick penetration move or space on the wing. This action may open up screen-and-roll action for the player who set the dribble block. For best results, use this option when the center (5) is on the opposite block.

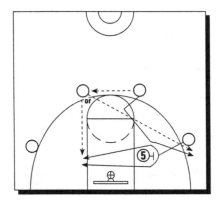

Diagram 6-7.

Diagram 6-8.

Diagram 6-9: We want to post up a forward. After passing to the corner, the passer goes behind the passcatcher for a hand-off. If 5 is opposite the ball, the forward cuts halfway across the lane, then buttonhooks back across the lane for post-up position and a pass from the corner.

Diagram 6-10: Same situation, except this time, the center (5) is on the same side as the ball. The passer goes behind the passcatcher for a hand-off. Notice the replacement action by the other perimeter players.

Diagram 6-11: Here's the continuation from Diagram 6-10. After handing the ball back to his teammate, the forward uses a screen by 5 to free himself up on the opposite block. On ball reversal, you have an ideal angle for passing the ball into the forward posting up.

Diagram 6-12: In order to continue the Flex Plus offense, we must fill, often by replacement action, two elbow and two corner positions on the perimeter. Again, here's a basic elbow-to-corner pass, followed by a cut to the basket and a quick screen across the lane.

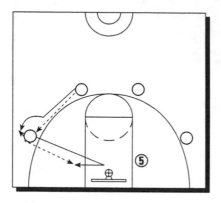

Diagram 6-9.

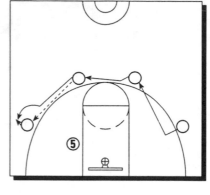

Diagram 6-10.

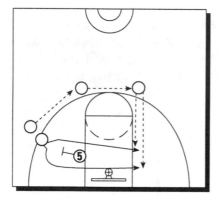

Diagram 6-11.

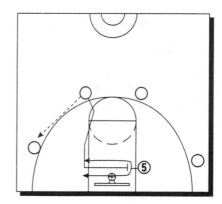

Diagram 6-12.

Diagram 6-13: Each perimeter player rotates one spot toward the ball to fill the vacant elbow area and each subsequent vacancy. The original cutter fills the weakside corner spot. You'll notice several keys. First, the player who screened across must clear the lane quickly to avoid a three-second violation. Second, his teammates on the perimeter don't just rotate toward the ball; they fake and get free. They move with a purpose. This same basic movement and action on the perimeter applies even when the center is on the ballside. In this case, the passer cuts to the opposite corner, and each perimeter player rotates toward the ball to achieve continuity. Once the pass goes back from the corner to the "new" player at the elbow, the offense starts anew.

Diagram 6-14: Another example of perimeter replacement action takes place on this elbow-to-elbow pass. Here, the forward in the corner opts to use the backpick by 5. The downscreener moves to the corner.

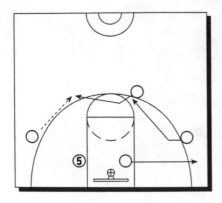

Diagram 6-13.

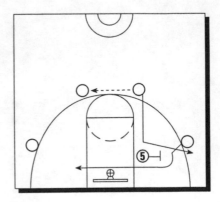

Diagram 6-14.

Diagram 6-15: The defense recognizes the action and takes away the options. The player with the ball dribbles elbow-to-elbow. A player moves from the corner to the vacated elbow area, and the cutter clears to the weakside corner to fill the perimeter spots. Again, this perimeter movement fills the need for two elbow and two corner players.

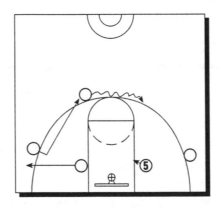

Diagram 6-15.

BACKDOOR OPPORTUNITIES AND CONTINUING THE OFFENSE

Diagram 6-16: With the center opposite the ball, a smart forward can beat an overplaying defender with a backdoor cut.

Diagram 6-17: If the backdoor cut isn't open, the elbow player dribbles to the corner to establish continuity and perimeter positioning. With a quick screen across, the original cutter may free up 5 for post-up action and a pass from the corner. The screener clears across the lane to the corner to fill a vacancy in the corner created when other perimeter players rotated.

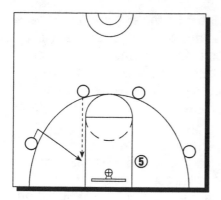

Diagram 6-16.

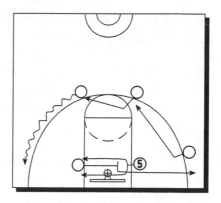

Diagram 6-17.

Diagram 6-18: The ball is in the corner after a pass and give-and-go cut from the elbow. The player at the opposite elbow fills the strongside elbow spot. If overplayed, he goes backdoor for a potential pass and shot.

Diagram 6-19: The defense overplays an elbow-to-elbow pass. The player at the weakside elbow goes backdoor, then clears to the corner away from the ball. The player in the weakside corner fills the vacated elbow position.

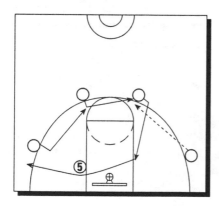

Diagram 6-18.

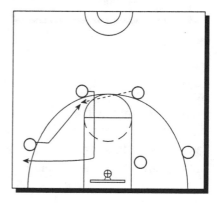

Diagram 6-19.

FLEX PLUS VERSUS SWITCHING DEFENSES

You must prepare for the possibility that your opponent will use a switching strategy to limit the effectiveness of your Flex Plus offense. Defenders occasionally switch responsibilities, especially on the downscreen action so common in Flex Plus. Switching defenses are vulnerable to a variety of options, as we'll demonstrate here. Note: Defenders are represented by Squares, designated A and B.

Diagram 6-20: The ball starts at the elbow opposite 5. On the elbow-to-elbow pass and downscreen, the corner player goes backdoor, then screens across the lane for 5. The player who downscreened fades to the corner for a potential jump shot or pass in to 5. Very often, the Defender A, who is guarding the downscreener, waits for a moment or two in the lane, anticipating a cut to the elbow by the forward coming out of the corner. This momentary lapse, created by a backdoor move, opens up a skip pass from the elbow to the corner.

Diagram 6-21: The ball starts at the elbow on the same side as 5. This time, instead of using the downscreen, the forward coming out of the corner chooses to use a backpick by 5. Again, Defender A is caught out of position anticipating an elbow cut. Often, both the skip pass and post pass are available.

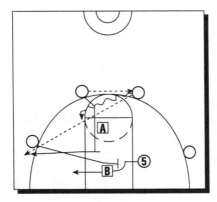

Diagram 6-20.

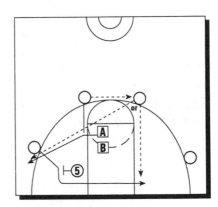

Diagram 6-21.

Diagram 6-22: When teammates know each other well, they can anticipate a switching strategy and defeat it with clever, unpatterned play. Here, after making an elbow-to-elbow pass, the passer moves as though he will set a textbook downscreen. Instead, he "slips" the screen and flashes back into an open area in the lane. If Defenders A and B both react to the cutter, the player coming out of the corner may be open at the elbow area for a high-percentage jump shot.

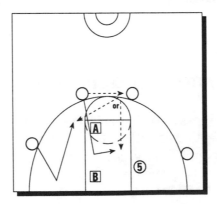

Diagram 6-22.

HOLD ACTION

No team wants to be too predictable. After running Flex Plus for several years, we saw an opportunity to install an option that presents a quick post-up opportunity for our center.

Diagram 6-23: The play starts in a routine fashion, with an elbow-to-elbow pass away from 5. The passer moves to set a downscreen, then flashes back to the elbow. The forward in the corner cuts off the screen by 5 for post-up action.

Diagram 6-24: If the defense anticipates and overplays the usual downscreen, the original passer will be open at the elbow area. On an elbow-to-elbow return pass, either a quick dump-in pass to 5, or the opportunity to dribble and improve the angle for a post pass, is available.

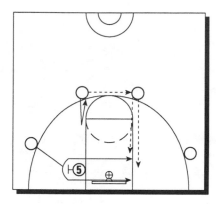

Diagram 6-23.

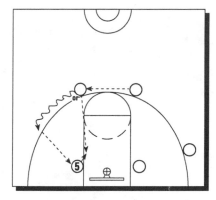

Diagram 6-24.

DRILLING FLEX PLUS

It takes plenty of "time well-spent" to install a continuity offense such as Flex Plus and run it effectively in games. Assuming you have the time and personnel, I suggest that you take a gradual approach in practice—teaching and coaching elements of the offense, and drilling the individual skills required to run it. I recommend lots of dummying, three-on-zero, four-on-zero and five-on-zero. Slowly introduce defense to the mix, increasing the defense's presence and intensity as your players demonstrate their individual and collective ability to understand and run the offense.

CHAPTER 7

Breakdown Offense: Motion

As you read in Chapter 6, I believe your team will enjoy its greatest success attacking man-to-man defenses with a mixture of set-play and breakdown strategies. In Chapter 6, we laid the groundwork for breakdown offense and introduced the College of Charleston's version of the Flex, called Flex Plus.

In this chapter, the topic is Motion offense—another continuity-style system that may be just what your team needs in breakdown situations. My first experience with Motion offense came as a player and coach at St. John's University. As Coach Lou Carnesecca's assistant, I got plenty of exposure to the model Motion offenses run by Bob Knight's Army and Indiana teams and Dean Smith's North Carolina Tar Heels. By attending clinics, watching their teams on television and videotape, and experiencing their systems first-hand as an opponent, I was able to digest Knight-style and Smith-style Motion offense. Believe me, when opposing Knight's and Smith's teams, you got plenty of food for thought.

To this day, both programs teach and demand excellent ball and player movement from their Motion attacks. North Carolina's version of Motion offense is characterized by calculated, but quick, ball and player movement. Knight's Motion offense is more physical, with hard, grinding screens as a building block for offense. Still, when it comes to Motion offense, North Carolina and Indiana speak the same language, even if they use different tones. Both teams start with the same principles and concepts, and their execution levels are similarly high. Both teams do a great job of reading defenses, using different options, and striking whenever they see a flaw or weakness.

MOTION OUR WAY

As a coach, I've worked long and hard to incorporate the best aspects of many coaches' Motion systems. Again, the fundamentals are the same. We merely interpret things our own way—looking to integrate various players' skills into a smooth-running system. At the College of Charleston, Motion offense emphasizes tremendous team play, timing, player movement (especially without the ball), and reading defenses. Spacing of players from 15 to 18 feet apart and court balance—two players in position to defend, three rebounding—are important elements of good Motion offense. Because each phase of the offense requires two- and three-player interaction, Motion offense needs space to operate.

While we as coaches "never say never," use of the dribble is minimal in our Motion offense. Our players use the bounce primarily to improve angles for passing, develop court balance, negate the five-second count, and penetrate to the basket.

Ball movement and reversal from one side of the court to the other keep the defense busy and continually recovering and adjusting. We encourage player movement on the weak side of the floor to occupy defenders and limit their ability to help teammates who are beaten.

On the perimeter, we encourage players to move aggressively without the ball to free themselves up as outlets for passes. Our perimeter players always have the option of a strong backdoor move without the ball to keep defenders honest and limit the effectiveness of high-pressure overplay. The ability to get open, teamed with catching the ball in classic "triple threat" position, makes perimeter players all the more effective.

FOUR-OUT, ONE-IN MOTION

One of the beauties of Motion offense is the ability it gives a coach to use his personnel to maximum advantage. From 1994 through 1997, the College of Charleston had the luxury of a dominant center, Thaddeous Delaney. Because we wanted Thad to operate around the basket, we played Four-Out, One-In Motion, with our big man inside and his four teammates on the perimeter.

During the same timeframe, Coach Rick Barnes was developing an upcoming powerhouse at Clemson University. In his early days at Clemson, Barnes didn't have a powerful center, but had a wealth of mobile, sharp-shooting perimeter players. Predictably enough, Barnes installed a Five-Out Motion attack with a wide open middle.

Two teams; two options.

In our Four-Out Motion, the center uses screens, flashes block-to-block, posts up when the ball is coming to his side of the floor, and sets backpicks, then flashes. Perimeter players must understand their roles and strengths. Some are better shooters; others are slasher/drivers; others still are great screeners, passers or rebounders. The basic movements for perimeter players are pass and cut (give and go), pass and screen away, set and use fade screens, and set backpicks.

FIVE-OUT MOTION

This is the purest form of basketball and the most difficult to defend. At the College of Charleston, we take the same perimeter principles we used in our Four-Out attack and empower five mobile players to use them. Nobody stands still. The ball and players are continually moving, with a wide open lane and post areas. The open middle is inviting for players who can use their quickness to cut to the basket or flash to post-up areas.

From a defensive perspective, this can be a nightmare. Big players are put in the unaccustomed role of guarding face-the-basket threats, which is hard enough for smaller, quicker players to do. By exploiting slow-footed opponents, you may force an opposing coach to change his lineup, sacrificing offensive power for defensive quickness. Certainly, a shotblocker can't simply camp out under the hoop, unless he's willing to surrender uncontested jump shots by capable shooters. In classic Five-Out Motion, your team's "center" may actually be more of a forward, with shooting range out to the three-point stripe.

BASIC GUIDELINES FOR MOTION OFFENSE

Aside from when to use it, personnel considerations, and spacing, the basic guidelines of Motion offense govern ball and player movement. When the ball is passed from one spot on the floor to another, prescribed cuts and screens occur. Within these movements are options and wrinkles that make a well-schooled Motion offense so difficult to defend.

Five basic guidelines govern the College of Charleston's Motion offense. These are:

- Pass and cut (give and go);

- Pass and screen away;

- Fade screen action;

- Backpick action, with the screener flashing to the ball; and

- Screening across the lane.

In the following diagrams, we illustrate these guidelines, including their variations.

DIAGRAMS OF BASIC MOTION ACTION

Let's use the actions of three perimeter players to illustrate some of the basic ball and player movement of the Motion offense. This is not only a good way to illustrate the basics of Motion; it's a great way to teach them—a few players at a time in practice.

Diagram 7-1: Here is pass-and-cut action. After the pass to the wing, the passer cuts to the basket for a give-and-go opportunity. Should the cutter be covered, another perimeter player has rotated to the top of the key as an outlet.

Diagram 7-2: Pass-and-screen-away action is self-descriptive. After passing, the passer looks to set a screen for a teammate on the weak side of the floor. The player using the screen has four options—a curl move, a backdoor move, a cut to the ball, and flare action. In this case, he curls around the screen, looking for a pass on the low block. Meanwhile, the screener pops back off the screen and replaces himself at the top of the key.

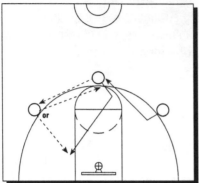

Diagram 7-1.

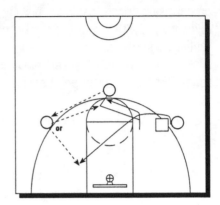

Diagram 7-2.

Diagram 7-3: As stated, pass-and-screen-away options vary according to how the weakside player uses the screen. Here, he goes backdoor, again looking for an entry pass on the low block. Again, the screener pops back as an outlet at the top of the key.

Diagram 7-4: Here's another option on pass-and-screen-away action. This time, the weakside player uses the screen to cut straight to the ball. With the slightest advantage, this may result in a high-percentage jump shot. This time, the screener replaces his teammate on the weak side, rather that popping back to what is essentially an occupied area. This maintains appropriate perimeter spacing and reduces defenders' opportunities to overplay the cutter.

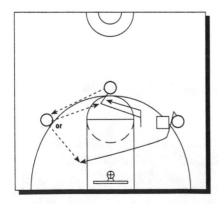

Diagram 7-3.

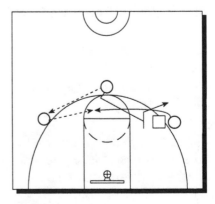

Diagram 7-4.

Diagram 7-5: Some defenders either can't or won't aggressively guard a player over the top of a screen. In this case, screen-away-and-flare action results in an open jump shot for a smart perimeter player. After the initial screen-away action, the weakside player flares behind the screener. An accurate pass, combined with the pass receiver catching the ball in triple-threat position, results in an open shot. One tip here: by lining up the screener directly between himself and the basket, the passcatcher makes it doubly difficult for a defender to contest a jump shot.

Diagram 7-6: Fade-screen action effectively reverses the players' roles after the initial pass. In this case, after making an initial pass, the passer uses a screen from a teammate on the weak side. The result, after a skip pass, is an open jump shot. Note that the screener steps out to the top of the key to re-establish court balance and serve as an option. Fade-screen action is particularly effective when the original passer is guarded very tightly, or his defender jumps to the ball on the initial pass to the wing.

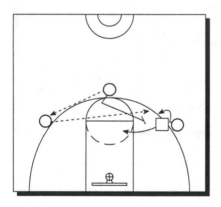

Diagram 7-5.

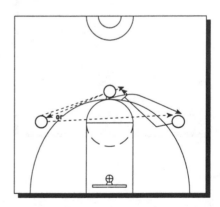

Diagram 7-6.

Diagram 7-7: The fade screen offers a simple but effective option, cutting all the way to the basket for a pass and layup.

Diagram 7-8: Backpick-and-flash action can be extremely effective. After passing from a low wing or corner position, the passer uses a backpick to make a curl or backdoor move to the basket. The screener then flashes to the ball, looking for a pass and short jump shot.

Diagram 7-9: Screen-across action builds on the initial pass-and-cut movement from the perimeter. After making an initial cut to the basket for a give-and-go opportunity, the cutter screens across the lane for a teammate cutting to the ballside block.

Diagram 7-10: This time, after the passer makes a backdoor cut to the basket, then the passer screens across the lane for a teammate.

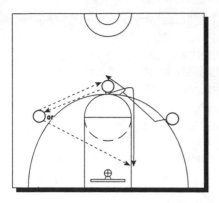

Diagram 7-7.

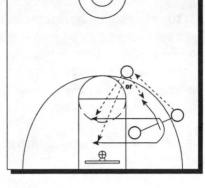

Diagram 7-8.

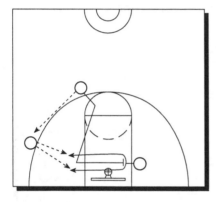

Diagram 7-9.

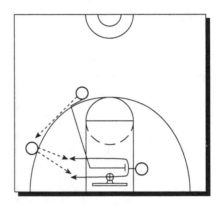

Diagram 7-10.

Diagrams 7-1 through 7-10 illustrate an important element of successful man-to-man offense. In most instances, players moving without the ball must work to gain an advantage. They must fake one way and go the other—or at least establish the possibility that they will change directions. In Diagram 7-9, the passer moves as though he may screen away, then cuts to the basket. In Diagram 7-10, the passer takes a step toward his teammate with the ball, then cuts backdoor to the basket.

DIAGRAMS OF FOUR-OUT, ONE-IN MOTION

Having diagrammed and described basic movements of perimeter players in our Motion offense, let's bring our center into the mix. If you have an effective center whose best work is done around the basket, you'll want to use Four-Out Motion for reasons described earlier in this chapter.

Isolating the Post

One way to bring your center (5) into the attack is through a number of ball and player movements that essentially isolate the post player.

Diagram 7-11: Ball reversal on the perimeter results in a post-up opportunity. Here, a block-to-block flash, accompanied by ball reversal, produces an excellent angle for an entry pass into the post. Notice that the perimeter players are using Motion principles—passing and screening, or passing and using screens.

Diagram 7-12: Instead of flashing from block to block, the center establishes post-up position, then waits for ball reversal to produce an effective angle for a pass inside.

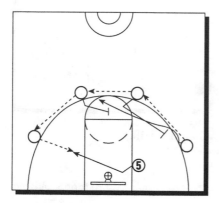

Diagram 7-11.

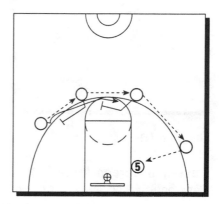

Diagram 7-12.

Diagram 7-13: A quick screen across the lane isolates the center (5) for a post-up opportunity. Again, it all comes within the Motion system, beginning with a pass and cut, continuing with the screen-across action, and resetting with potential outlets through an effective rotation on the perimeter.

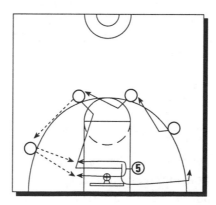

Diagram 7-13.

Pass-and-Cut Action

Diagram 7-14: This diagram illustrates a "rule within a rule." Following a lateral pass across the top of the key, the passer fakes screen-away action and cuts to the basket for give-and-go action. Notice that the cutter does not move to an occupied post area.

Diagram 7-15: The same "rule within a rule" applies on this penetrating pass to the wing area. Don't cut to an occupied post area.

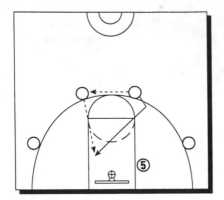

Diagram 7-14.

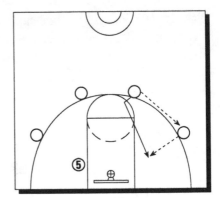

Diagram 7-15.

Pass-and-Screen-Away Action

Pass-and-Screen-Away action describes a single element of Motion offense. Within that element are four options, to be explored by the player using the screen. They are: curl move, backdoor cut, cutting straight to the ball, and flare action.

Diagram 7-16: After the initial pass to the wing, the passer screens away. His teammate curls around the screen, looking for a scoring pass from the wing. The screener then pops back to the top of the key, effectively replacing himself as an outlet if needed and providing court balance.

Diagram 7-17: After the initial pass to the wing, the passer screens away. His teammate makes a backdoor cut to the unoccupied post, looking for a scoring pass from the wing. The screener then pops back to the top of the key, effectively replacing himself as an outlet if needed and providing court balance.

Diagram 7-18: After the initial pass to the wing, the passer screens away. His teammate cuts to the ball, looking for a scoring pass from the wing. In this case, the screener then replaces his teammate on the weak side of the floor.

Diagram 7-19: After the initial pass to the wing, the passer screens away. His teammate uses flare action, looking for a scoring pass from the wing. Notice two keys here: in moving without the ball, the pass receiver 1) fakes a backdoor cut before making a flare move, and 2) tries to align himself so that the screener stands directly between him and the basket.

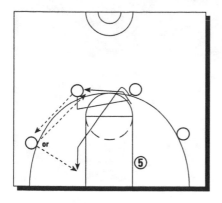

Diagram 7-16.

Diagram 7-17.

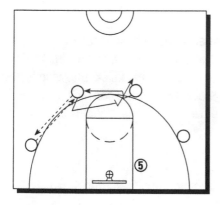

Diagram 7-18.

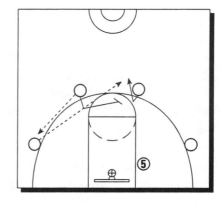

Diagram 7-19.

Fade-Screen Action

Fade-Screen action is an effective alternative, especially if the passer has established pass-and-cut and pass-and-screen-away action in previous possessions. To maximize its effectiveness, the player setting the fade screen should be the last player on his side of the court, and your players should use fade-screen action on the side of the floor opposite the post.

Diagram 7-20: After passing the ball, the passer uses a fade screen from his teammate on the wing. Here, the player using the screen is looking for a jump shot or a catch-and-drive. The screener pops back to the top of the key for court balance.

Diagram 7-21: After passing the ball, the passer uses a fade screen from his teammate on the wing. Here, the player using the screen makes a basket cut, looking for a catch-and-layup. The screener pops back to the top of the key for court balance.

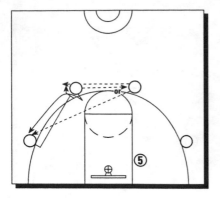

Diagram 7-20.

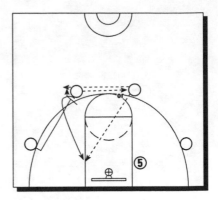

Diagram 7-21.

Backpick Action
Diagram 7-22: Here's a classic center-backpick scenario, resulting in three high-percentage opportunities. The offensive player in the corner passes to a teammate on the perimeter, initiating ball reversal. The center (5) sets a backpick, allowing his teammate to curl or go backdoor to the opposite block. Should the center's defender attempt to help out on the cutter, the center may be open on a flash into the lane.

Screen-Across Action for the Center
Classic Four-Out Motion offense puts the center (5) in position to screen and use screens.

Diagram 7-23: After the initial pass-and-cut to the unoccupied post, the cutter screens across the lane for 5. 5 cuts to the low post, looking for a scoring pass from the wing area. Note the perimeter rotation, with players, including the cutter-screener, filling the four perimeter spots for court balance.

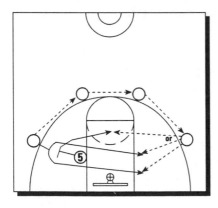

Diagram 7-22.

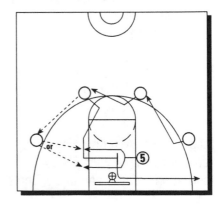

Diagram 7-23.

BACKDOOR CUTS

Backdoor cuts by perimeter players are a big part of Motion offense. The backdoor cut gives defenders one more thing to think about and limits their ability to overplay perimeter players. If the backdoor cut is intended to set up a score, it must be away from the post occupied by the center (5). However, even if the center is in the post area, a backdoor cut can be an effective means of clearing defenders away from a certain spot on the court.

Diagram 7-24: Here's a backdoor cut from the top of the perimeter. The passer takes a step toward the ball, then cuts to an unoccupied post. If he does not receive a return pass, the cutter screens across the lane for the center, then rotates back to the unoccupied spot on the weak side of the perimeter.

Diagram 7-25: The backdoor cut from the corner takes advantage of an overplaying defender and establishes an ideal angle for screen-across action. If the pass is not made to the cutter, the cutter screens across and the ballhandler dribbles to the vacated spot on the perimeter. The dribble serves two purposes: it improves the ballhandler's angle for a pass into 5 on the low post, and it re-establishes perimeter balance.

Diagram 7-26: On a backdoor cut from the top of the perimeter, the cutter may clear through to either side of the floor. Here, he clears to the corner opposite the ball for better court balance.

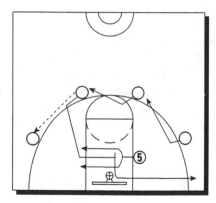

Diagram 7-24.

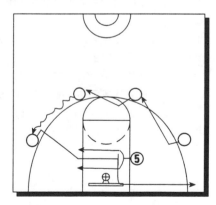

Diagram 7-25.

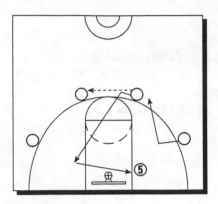

Diagram 7-26.

MOTION VERSUS SWITCHING DEFENSES

When employing an offense that encourages players to set and use a variety of perimeter and interior screens, you must anticipate that your opponent will consider a defensive strategy that includes "X" amount of switching. Earlier in this book, we discussed the importance of knowing not only your opponent's basic defensive set-up, but the tendencies within that defense. You gain this knowledge through scouting, through the experience of having played the same opponent previously, and by simple observation throughout a game.

This having been said, how do you discourage opponents from switching defensive assignments in screening situations?

Diagram 7-27: Blocks A and B represent defenders in a pass-and-screen-away situation. After the pass across the key, the passer looks to screen away. A and B anticipate the screen and move to switch assignments. Recognizing the potential switch, the screener moves to a position roughly halfway between the defenders, then "slips" the screen and makes a cut to the basket. This creates two options for the next pass—a look to the basket, where the cutter should have an advantage on Defender B, or a pass on the perimeter.

Diagram 7-28: The player coming out of the corner is about to set a fade screen for the player who just passed the ball. Anticipating a switch, he "slips" the screen, cutting between Defenders A and B toward the basket. This time, Defender A figures to be at a disadvantage in attempting to cover the cutter. This creates two options for the next pass—a look to the basket, or a pass on the perimeter.

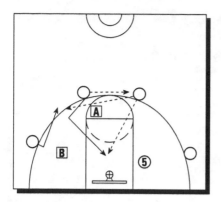

Diagram 7-27.

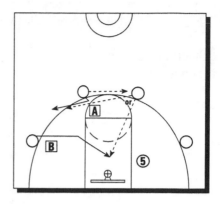

Diagram 7-28.

DIAGRAMS OF FIVE-OUT MOTION

With the exception of the unoccupied post, many of the same principles apply in Five-Out Motion. The next eight diagrams show ball-and-player movement common in a Five-Out set. Remember, if you lack a strong inside player, or if you simply have a handful of quick, sharp-shooting perimeter-type players, Five-Out Motion may be the system for you. In general, your five players will occupy two corners, two wings and the top-of-the-key area.

Diagram 7-29: Pass-and-cut action is available to any perimeter player. Rotation and replacement assure court balance and continued ball and player movement.

Diagram 7-30: Here, pass-and-screen-away action results in a curl cut into the lane. Should he not receive a pass, the cutter will be most effective by clearing to the perimeter corner opposite the ball. After screening, the original passer pops back to the top of the key. The corner player moves up to a wing area. Once again, balance results.

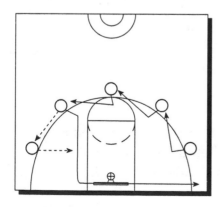

Diagram 7-29.

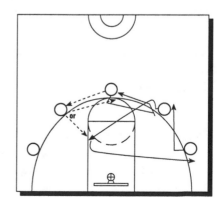

Diagram 7-30.

Diagram 7-31: The same action applies on a backdoor cut.

Diagram 7-32: Should the cutter move straight to the ball, the offense regains balance with the screener simply replacing the cutter in the wing area.

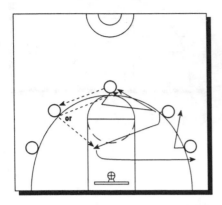

Diagram 7-31.

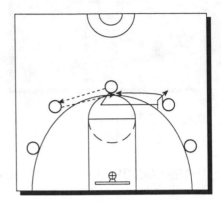

Diagram 7-32.

Diagram 7-33: Here's flare action after pass-and-screen-away movement.

Diagram 7-34: The fade screen produces a jump shot or dribble-drive opportunity. Notice that the screener steps out to a wing position to restore perimeter balance.

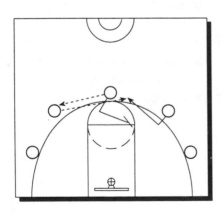

Diagram 7-33.

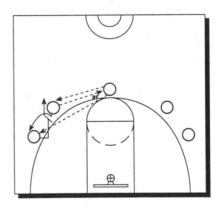

Diagram 7-34.

Diagram 7-35: Here, the original passer uses a fade screen to free himself for a basket cut and layup. Because this move is less likely to be open, it's particularly important that the screener establish himself as an outlet on the wing of a balanced perimeter.

Diagram 7-36: Because the post area is open, perimeter defenders may not anticipate backpicks and screens. Here, after the pass-and-cut move, the cutter clears to the corner opposite the ball. Along the way, he sets a surprise backpick for a teammate coming across the lane for post-up position.

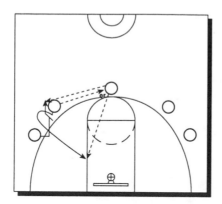

Diagram 7-35.

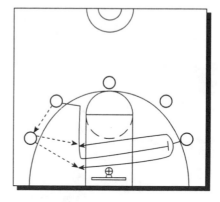

Diagram 7-36.

The open middle inherent in Five-Out Motion places a premium on give-and-goes, backdoor cuts, and slipping screens. The first priority offensively is always a strong cut or move for a layup. By using the same principles demonstrated in the previous section on Four-Out Motion, you can take advantage of overplaying and switching defenses.

CHAPTER 8

Three-Point Shots: Hitting the Home Run

If you were to ask me the three most significant developments in basketball over the last four decades, I would cite:

- The sheer size and athleticism of players—big guys who can really move;

- The installation of a shot clock at the professional and college levels; and

- The acceptance of the three-point shot at all levels—pro, college, high school and recreational.

Like it or hate it, the three-point shot—the home run of basketball—is here to stay. Along with it come significant impacts on general and situational strategies.

First and foremost, the three-point shot alters the fundamental mathematics of the game. Hitting 40% of your three-point attempts is equivalent to hitting 60% of your twos. That percentage would have busted a game wide open in the "old days."

"Time and score" considerations are also much more complicated. The concept of the "safe" lead has changed. Before the installation of a three-point shot, coaches breathed the proverbial sigh of relief much earlier in games. If you had a three-point lead in the final seconds, you'd tell your players not to foul. Now, you must contest three-point shots, or risk facing overtime. Worse yet, in contesting the shot, you run the risk of surrendering a four-point play (three-pointer plus a foul shot) and losing in regulation. I've been there, and it hurts.

Given these and less obvious factors, it's no surprise that more and more teams are employing man-to-man as their defense of choice. Of course, man-to-man is the rule at the pro level. But at the college level, where some players are future pros and the three-point stripe is closer to the basket, man-to-man is increasingly prevalent. As a coach who favors use of multiple defenses, I have grown more inclined to use man-to-man defense throughout a game. When I do use a zone, it's a matchup, coupling aggressive man-to-man principles with basic zone tenets. The reason: I don't want our team to surrender uncontested three-point shots. As a coach, you probably feel the same way.

If it isn't a whole new ballgame, it's certainly a different game, as the following examples demonstrate. Game One of the 1995 NBA championship series between the Houston Rockets and the Orlando Magic yielded game, team and individual records for three-point shooting. The teams combined to attempt 62 three-pointers. The Rockets, who were 14-of-32 from three-point range, set marks for three-pointers attempted and made by one team. Houston guard Kenny Smith made seven threes, an NBA Finals record.

Just one year later, the Rockets were again involved in an NBA-playoff, record-setting three-point barrage—this time on the losing side. The Seattle Sonics made 20 of 27 three-point shot attempts in their second-round, Game Two victory over the soon-to-be-dethroned champions. What makes these examples even more startling is that NBA teams are required, by rule, to play man-to-man defense, which should limit three-point attempts and percentage.

At the college level, where zone defense is allowed but less and less popular, the University of Kentucky Wildcats are among the more visible and effective proponents of the three-point shot. Under Coach Rick Pitino, who has since moved on to the NBA's Boston Celtics, Kentucky used the three-pointer as the high-octane fuel for a point-scoring machine. During its 1996 national championship run, Kentucky attempted 573 three-point shots, hitting 222, for a .387 shooting percentage. More impressive still, Kentucky connected on 44 of 97 attempts (.454 accuracy) during the NCAA Tournament.

In 1997, Arizona dethroned Kentucky as NCAA champion. While the western Wildcats weren't as prolific from the three-point stripe as their eastern brethren, they connected on at least one three-pointer that was a dagger in this coach's heart. In the second round of the NCAA Tournament, Arizona defeated College of Charleston, 73-69. In an exciting, hotly contested game, the biggest shot of all may have been a three-pointer Arizona freshman Michael Bibby hit in the final minute. You lose track of a great shooter for a split second, and he'll kill you, three points at a time.

High school coaches should understand that the three-point shot can affect their teams just as much, even if prep-level players aren't generally the type of shooters you see at the college level. For example, during the 1986-87 season, the Palmer (Iowa) High School team made 210 of 396 three-point attempts—a whopping 53% accuracy figure. I know a couple hundred college coaches who would take that kind of shooting anytime.

My first experience with the three-point shot came during the early 1970s, when I spent three seasons as assistant coach of the American Basketball Association's New York Nets. In the battle for the entertainment dollar, the ABA pioneered the three-point shot, with some occasionally wild results. A new role, three-point specialist, was created and filled by such long-range bombers as Rick Mount, Fred Lewis, Darrell Carrier, Lou Dampier and Bob Verga. For the Nets, Rick Barry once hit seven three-pointers in a row, and John Roche won several games, including a pivotal playoff game against the Kentucky Colonels, with his long-range bombs.

And they truly were bombs. By comparison, the 19-foot, 9-inch three-pointer used at the college and high school levels is a very makeable shot. So, why not use it?

As a coach, the ball's in your court. Before your team can take maximum advantage of the three-point shot, you must identify players who can hit the shot consistently, then arm them with an offensive system that creates openings.

It starts with a simple enough piece of advice: Know your personnel. Three-point shots are for three-point shooters, not for players who have trouble hitting 15-footers. Communicate clearly to your players who has the green light, and, perhaps more importantly, who does not.

Once you've determined which players can hit the three-pointer, give them some basic rules. First, a player should never look at his feet in relation to the three-point stripe after catching a pass. This momentary lapse allows defenders to recover and disrupts a shooter's natural timing and stroke. Second, unless time and score considerations demand it, a player should never attempt a three-point shot with a defender draped all over him.

The purpose of these guidelines is to assure that the three-point shot is an asset, not a debit. You want to incorporate the three-pointer into your arsenal only if it achieves positive ends—spreading the defense for inside action, and increasing your points-per-possession.

Once you've established these basics, it's time to install a system for generating three-point opportunities. If you've given some thought to the set plays and breakdown offenses presented in the preceding four chapters, you've realized that many of these offenses create three-point options. The key issues are appropriate spacing, setting and using screens, ball reversal, and spotting up for threes instead of twos. You may even wish to call a play "for three"—encouraging a shooter or shooters to look specifically for three-point shots.

Your players should also understand that some of the best three-point opportunities come outside of the system, via opportunity basketball. Transition play offers good three-point opportunities to the team willing to explore them. The reasons are fairly obvious. When the offensive team has "the numbers," the defending team generally will build from the basket out. This implies three-point openings for players running the wings, or trailers, coming into the play late. An open-minded coach does not discourage his best shooters from looking for and launching the occasional three-point shot, even with a numerical advantage in transition.

When the attacking team doesn't have a numerical advantage, it still may have an organizational edge in transition. How often have you seen a defender "lose" the player he is guarding in transition? With a smart point guard handling the ball and a confident shooter moving to an open spot on the floor, the result can be a quick three-pointer in transition.

Another opening for three-point shots against man-to-man defense comes as the result of inside-out action. Establish your inside game early, through good execution of your offensive gameplan, and many teams will resort to double-teaming your post players. A smart perimeter player reads the double-team, spots up in an open area and calls for the ball. When the post player passes the ball back outside, the result can be an uncontested or modestly contested three-point shot.

One other opportunity is actually a double-edged sword. When you incorporate the three-point shot into your offense, your players must be aware of the risks and rewards of long rebounds. Quite often, a missed three-point attempt will result in an uncharacteristically long or high rebound. In your team's hands, these wild caroms can be converted into an opportunity jump shot, or, better yet, passed back inside for layups. In your opponents' hands, a long rebound can spell quick transition the other way.

Having reviewed these general principles, here are some three-point plays to consider. They may be useful either as established parts of your set play offense, or as situational plays, late in a quarter or game, when you want or need a three-point shot.

Play No. 1

In all likelihood, your best three-point shooters will be your two guards and small forward. Conversely, your power forward and center, may be more effective as screen-setters. Play No. 1 employs players in their natural roles—a real plus at crunch time.

Diagram 8-1: 1 dribbles to the frontcourt and passes to 3, stepping to the top of the key. 1 and 2 then use screens by 4 and 5 to fade to three-point spots on the wings. If open, 3 can turn and shoot. If covered, he can pass to 1 or 2 for a jump shot.

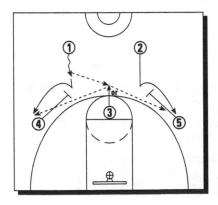

Diagram 8-1.

Play No. 2

Fundamentally the same action as Play No. 1, this play employs 2 as the initiator in place of 1, and 1 as the initial passcatcher in place of 3.

Diagram 8-2: 2 dribbles to the frontcourt and passes to 1, stepping to the top of the key. 2 and 3 then use screens by 4 and 5 to fade to three-point spots on the wings. If open, 1 can turn and shoot. If covered, he can pass to 2 or 3 for a jump shot.

Diagram 8-3: If the first three options are unavailable, 4 and 5 set high dribble blocks for 1. 2 and 3 continue to fade toward the corners of the floor. 1 dribbles either way off a dribble block. 1's options are a quick shot or a pass to the ballside wing.

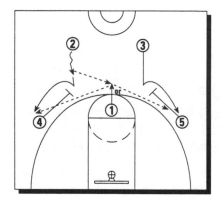

Diagram 8-2.

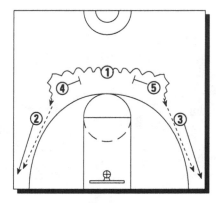

Diagram 8-3.

Play No. 3

This play offers several options, generated first by a high dribble block, then by staggered fade screens off the ball. Taken to its logical conclusion, Play No. 3 produces an open shot by your shooting guard, who figures to be your best three-point shooter.

Diagram 8-4: 1 initiates the offense, dribbling left, then right, around a dribble block by 2. 4 and 5 move to set screens on the opposite side of the floor. 1 may have a quick opening for shot. 3 may also be open for a jump shot from the corner.

Diagram 8-5: 4 and 5 screen for 2, who loops around the screens to a spot on the wing. 1 passes crosscourt to 2 for a three-point shot.

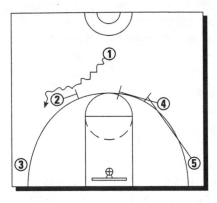

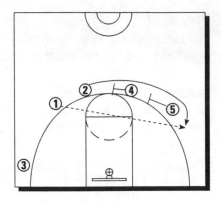

Diagram 8-4.   **Diagram 8-5.**

Play No. 4

Here's a great play to free up your shooting guard. The screen-for-the-screener action, capped off by a big-for-small screen, is an effective way to produce three-point shots.

Diagram 8-6: 1 initiates by dribbling from left to right toward a wing area. 2 screens diagonally for 5, setting up a situation in which 2's defender may choose to help out inside. 4 then screens for 2, who cuts to a three-point area on the right side of the key. 1 passes to 2 for a three-point shot.

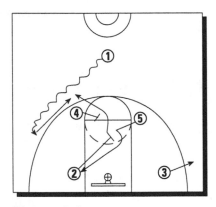

Diagram 8-6.

Play No. 5

Some of the principles involved in Play No. 4 work here as well. 3's involvement as a screener initially establishes 5 as a more credible decoy. It also establishes a staggered-screen situation for 2.

Diagram 8-7: 1 initiates by dribbling from left to right toward a wing area. 3 sets a backscreen for 5. 2 also screens for 5. 5 cuts to the low block on the ballside.

Diagram 8-8: After completing his initial screen, 2 loops around staggered screens by 3 and 4 to a three-point area on the right side of the key. 1 passes to 2 for a three-point shot.

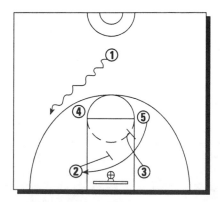

Diagram 8-7.

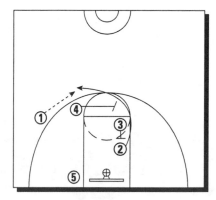

Diagram 8-8.

Play No. 6

This play presents a series of three-point options to a well-schooled team. Part of its beauty is that it originates from a UCLA set and action, similar to that described in Chapter 4. Ultimately, 1 may use a single or double screen to find an opening for a three-point shot.

Diagram 8-9: 1 dribbles right to left, then passes to 3, cutting to a wing area. 3 may have an immediate opening for a three-point shot. 1 cuts off a screen by 5.

Diagram 8-10: On the pass from 3 to 5, 4 screens down for 2, who moves to the top of the key. 1 steps toward the lane.

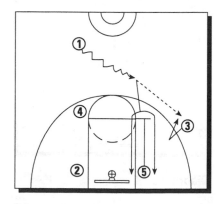

Diagram 8-9.

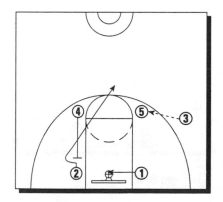

Diagram 8-10.

Diagram 8-11: 5 passes to 2, who may be open for a three-pointer. Meanwhile, 1 has the option of using a single screen by 4, or a double screen by 3 and 5 to find an opening on a wing area. 2 passes to 1 for a three-point shot.

Diagram 8-11.

Play No. 7
When you're trailing late in a game, time becomes a major factor. Here's a quick hitter, using big-for-small screens to free up three-point shooters in high-percentage areas.

Diagram 8-12: 1 dribbles to the top of the key. 2 and 3 criss-cross on the baseline, using screens by 4 and 5 to free themselves up on the wings. 1 takes a three-point shot, or passes to 2 or 3 for a three-point shot.

Diagram 8-13: Here's an option. Instead of criss-crossing, 2-3 fake the baseline move, then pop out to three-point areas on the wings. 1 can shoot the three-pointer, or penetrate and kick the ball to a three-point shooter on either wing.

Diagram 8-12.

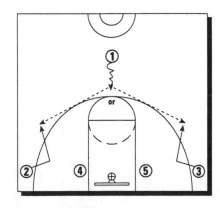

Diagram 8-13.

CHAPTER 9

Inbounding the Ball:
Another Way to Beat the Defense

By now, you're well aware of all the reasons why many teams prefer man-to-man defense to zone defense in a half-court setting. Man-to-man defense offers distinct advantages on the perimeter, where it doesn't concede open jump shots. This is especially important with the advent of a makeable three-point field goal. Under the basket, man-to-man defense includes specific defensive rebounding assignments, reducing opponents' stickback baskets.

Why, then, do some coaches prefer and switch to zone defenses when their opponents are inbounding the ball in the frontcourt?

Former Marquette University coach and current CBS-TV college basketball analyst Al McGuire makes a simple case for the zone. McGuire reasons that man-to-man defenses are particularly vulnerable to the quick screens and passes teams use when inbounding the ball. Why subject your team to quick-hitting, high-percentage inbound plays, when a zone can take away those primary options?

Historically, many coaches have agreed with this philosophy. However, a growing number of coaches deploy their teams in man-to-man defense when facing an opponent's frontcourt inbound plays. These coaches are willing to risk an opponent connecting on an occasional quick-hitter in exchange for all of the benefits man-to-man defense offers. If a defending team takes away the initial quick hitters with preparation and smart play, it forces the inbounding team to go to a non-threatening outlet, then attack a tough, half-court man-to-man defense.

I don't disagree with this thinking. However, if you think about it, your opponent choosing man-to-man defense in these situations represents a golden opportunity for your well-schooled players. In any given game, your team will inbound the ball in the frontcourt a dozen times or more. Our system of screens, player movement and quick passes will help you capitalize on these opportunities for high-percentage shots and easy baskets.

Here's what I mean.

First and foremost, thanks to a stoppage in play, the attacking team can catch its breath, check time and score, substitute as desired, decide which play to call, then initiate from a spot on the floor as little as 10 to 12 feet from the basket. There's no need to dribble up the floor against pressure just to initiate an attack. The point guard doesn't necessarily have to initiate the offense. In a very real sense, we've penetrated to a vulnerable area in the defense. From there, we can use any player, tall or small, to inbound the ball. These factors give us an immediate advantage.

Think of it from the defenders' perspective. The opponent starts from an ideal position with a multitude of options. Given where the play is initiated, the "ball-you-man" principle of man-to-man defense takes a real beating. Often, defenders don't realize they've been screened or beaten until the ball is in the basket. By then, it's too late for teammates, who have their own assignments, to offer much help.

In this chapter, I'll detail 16 plays, complete with options, for inbounding the ball in the frontcourt. Most originate on the baseline on either side of the lane. Because the game occasionally presents wrinkles, I'll show you a play that originates from the corner—often a tough place to inbound the ball. I'll also show my favorite sideline inbounds play, with its many attractive options.

Again, as I've said earlier in this book, you may not need or want all of these options. Pick and choose your favorites. Install them as you would any other half-court play, then use them with confidence in a game. Click often enough on your inbounding opportunities, and you'll see that execution in these critical situations will put your team over the top in close games.

Important note: In our system, these plays begin with the inbounder taking the ball from the official on a spot, slapping the ball to initiate action, then passing the ball. Cuts and screens begin with the initial ball-slap, and continue on the flight of the pass.

INBOUNDING ON THE BASELINE

Attacking teams face this opportunity many times during a game, whether as the result of a common foul, an opponent's violation, or because the ball has been passed or tipped across the baseline. For the purpose of this book, I'll assign these plays numbers, although you may call them by any name or number you wish.

Play No. 1
This play creates excellent outside-inside-outside options. It begins with a quick big-for-small upscreen and jump shot, continues with screen-for-the-screener action inside, and culminates with ball reversal for a jump shot.

Diagram 9-1: 4 screens up the lane from the ballside low block, freeing 2 for a jump shot on the wing. 5 screens diagonally for 4, who cuts to the weakside block. 5 rolls to the ballside block after the screen. 3 replaces 2.

Diagram 9-2: If the ball is inbounded to 2, he can take an open shot or look for 5 on a quick post-up move. If these options are not available, 2 reverses the ball through 3 to 1, who uses a screen by 4 to get open on the wing. 1 may also look inside to 4 posting up.

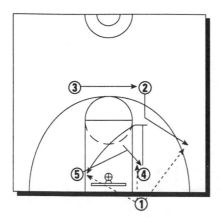

Diagram 9-1.

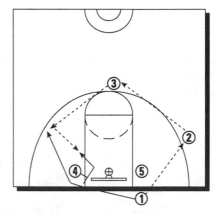

Diagram 9-2.

Play No. 2

Play No. 1 demonstrated the potential effectiveness of the inbounder using a screen to find an open spot on the floor. After several inside opportunities, Play No. 2 allows the inbounder the "pick his spot" on either side of the floor.

Diagram 9-3: 4 cuts of screens by 3 and 5 for a pass from 2 and potential layup. 3 then uses 5's screen to free himself in the corner.

Diagram 9-4: If the initial pass to 4 is unavailable, 2 passes to 3. 3's options include a jump shot or a pass inside to 5 posting up. 2 steps toward the middle of the floor, under the basket.

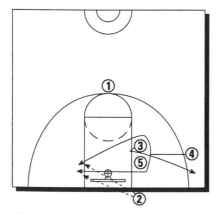

Diagram 9-3.

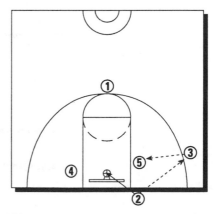

Diagram 9-4.

Diagram 9-5: Here's an effective play for 2. Instead of shooting or passing inside to 5, 3 passes to 1 at the top of the key. 2 then cuts to either wing, using a single screen by 4 for a jump shot or dump-in pass to 4, or staggered screens by 5 and 3 for a jump shot. 1 passes to 2.

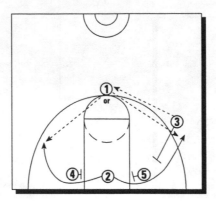

Diagram 9-5.

Play No. 3

This play has been very good to College of Charleston over the years. In 1991, we used it against North Carolina-Asheville to create a game-winning shot by a guard in the waning seconds. While that is an excellent option, you'll see that Play No. 3 also creates inside openings for your big players, 4 and 5.

Diagram 9-6: 2 sets a diagonal screen for 4, then uses a screen by 5 to free himself up for a jump shot on the ballside baseline. After screening, 5 spins back for inside position. 1 inbounds to 4, 5 or 2. 3 balances the floor.

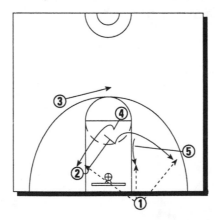

Diagram 9-6.

Play No. 4

Working from a similar set, this play brings 3 into the mix as a potential option.

Diagram 9-7: 2 sets an upscreen for 3, cutting down the weak side of the lane, then uses staggered screens by 4 and 5 to free himself up for a jump shot on the ballside baseline. After setting screens, 4 and 5 roll to open areas on the interior of the defense. 1 inbounds to 3, 4, 5 or 2.

Play No. 5

Starting with Play No. 5, here are four effective options off a set we call Double. The key is the various actions in and around a double screen. As you'll see, 2 and 3 can exchange roles in these plays. 1 always inbounds the ball; 4 and 5 always set a double screen.

In Play No. 5, the double screen is a decoy. The potential use of a double screen may confuse defenders, dividing their attention and opening up a quick hitter after a screen across the lane.

Diagram 9-8: 5 and 4 set themselves in position to set a double screen. Instead of using that screen, 3 uses a screen across the lane by 2 to establish position for a high-percentage scoring opportunity. 1 inbounds to 3.

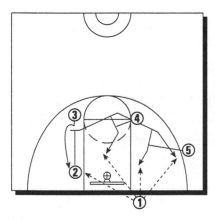

Diagram 9-7.

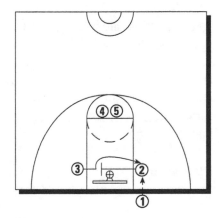

Diagram 9-8.

Play No. 6

This time, 2 uses the double screen for a jump shot.

Diagram 9-9: Instead of screening across, 3 steps out to the wing. 2 cuts around the double screen by 4 and 5. 1 inbounds to 3, who passes to 2 for a jump shot. Note: Should the first option not be available, 4 and 5 must clear the lane quickly to avoid being whistled for a three-second violation.

Play No. 7

In Play No. 5, 3 uses a screen across by 2. Here, 3 fakes across the lane, then cuts around the double screen to an opening.

Diagram 9-10: 2 steps across, as if to screen for 3. 4 and 5 set a double screen inside the foul line. 3 cuts around the double screen. 1 inbounds to 3 for a jump shot.

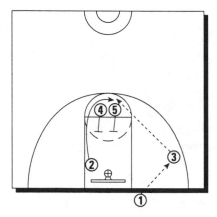

Diagram 9-9.

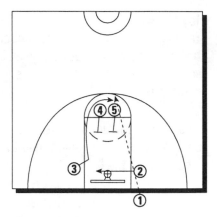

Diagram 9-10.

Play No. 8

To this point, 4 and 5 have been screeners. Here, an interior player uses a screen to cut to the block.

Diagram 9-11: Instead of stopping to receive a pass near the top of the key, 3 continues to a ballside wing area. 1 inbounds to 3. On the pass from 1 to 3, 5 screens for 4, who cuts to the block for pass from 3 and scoring opportunity. Note: 4 and 5 may exchange rolls on this play, depending on their individual skills and matchups.

Play No. 9

Here's a play that generates a quick jump shot for two or three points.

Diagram 9-12: 4, 2 and 5 set up at the foul line. 3 cuts to an open area on the ballside wing. On the pass from 1 to 3, 4 and 5 step into the lane, forming a double screen for 2. 2 steps back to the top of key. 3 passes to 2 for a jump shot.

Play No. 10

Lob passes are an effective weapon when inbounding the ball to a big player. To make this play and the next one work, you'll need two interior players who can set screens, catch lob passes and finish in traffic. Also, your designated inbounder must have the judgment and touch to throw an effective lob pass in heavy traffic.

Although many people think of lob passes being finished with a slam dunk, these plays seldom produce that clear an advantage. They are designed to create layups and high-percentage opportunities, not necessarily dunks. This means that you don't necessarily need a high flyer to use these plays—just execution and the strength to finish with opposing defenders nearby.

Diagram 9-13: The slap of the ball initiates two screens. Inside, 5 screens for 4, who fakes a quick move to the basket, then cuts out around the screen. Out top, 3 screens for 2, who moves to a ballside wing area as an outlet. 1 passes to 4 or 2.

Play No. 11

Once you've run Play No. 10, this play opens up, producing a direct pass to 5. One reason this simple action may be available is that interior defenders, having seen Play No. 10, may decide to switch defensive assignments the next time they sense that play is coming. If the interior defenders do switch, 5 often will find excellent inside position to catch and finish a lob.

Diagram 9-14: 4 fakes into the lane, then clears away from the play. 3 screens across for 2. 1 lobs to 5 or outlets to 2.

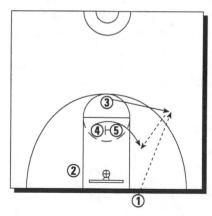

Diagram 9-11.

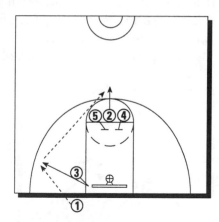

Diagram 9-12.

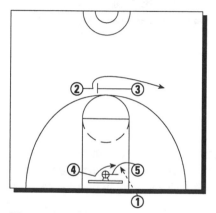

Diagram 9-13.

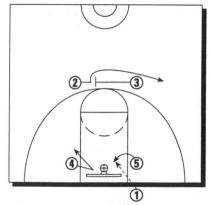

Diagram 9-14.

Play No. 12

These next three plays create openings for a versatile wing player, either 2 or 3. We'll show you how they work with 3 as a primary option. Should you prefer 2 in that role, simply invert 2 and 3 in the initial set. Either way, this play's effectiveness is based in large part on the choices it creates for a good scorer. Over the years, I've found that the more options a defender must cover, the less effective he is. Here, we give 3 two excellent options, one of which will generally be available.

Diagram 9-15: 2 screens up the lane for 3. 3 can go either way off the screen. He can cut to the ballside wing for a jump shot, or go to the weak side of the floor, using a double screen by 4 and 5 to free himself up under the basket. 1 passes to 3 for a jump shot or layup. 4 cuts to the basket after setting the double screen, using a brush screen from 5.

Play No. 13

If a defender thinks that 2 is a screener, he may fall asleep and let 2 gain an advantage on screen-and-roll action. The same thinking applies to 4 and his defender.

Diagram 9-16: 3 uses 2's upscreen to free himself up on the wing. 2 rolls to the weak side, using a double screen by 4 and 5. 4 cuts to the basket after setting the screen. 1 passes to 3 for a jump shot, 2 for a layup or 4 for an inside opportunity. 4 cuts to the basket after setting the double screen, using a brush screen from 5.

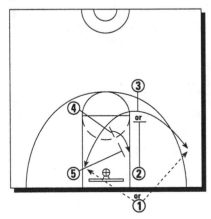

Diagram 9-15.

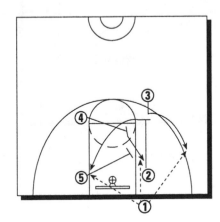

Diagram 9-16.

Play No. 14

Of course, 2 may roll either way. Here's another option.

Diagram 9-17: 3 uses 2's upscreen and a double screen by 4 and 5 to find an opening under the basket. 2 rolls to the wing for a jump shot. 4 cuts to the strongside block for a layup or power move. 1 passes to 2 for a jump shot, 3 for a layup or 4 for an inside opportunity.

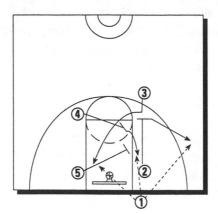

Diagram 9-17.

INBOUNDING FROM THE CORNER

It doesn't happen often, but the reality is that once or twice a game the officials will award your team the ball in or near a corner of the floor. This is not an optimal spot in terms of creating an immediate scoring opportunity. To the contrary, it sets the defense in what amounts to perfect trapping position. Imagine yourself as a ballhandler trapped in a corner without a dribble. This is what the inbounder faces.

In this challenging situation, your priority must be getting the ball inbounds, not creating a scoring opportunity. We look to create outlets, using screens and roll action to free up players at appropriate, well-spaced positions on the court.

Play No. 15
Diagram 9-18: On the slap of the ball, 1 screens across the lane for 3, then loops around a downscreen by 4 and a screen by 5 to an open area on the strong side of the court. After setting a screen, 5 retreats to an opening near midcourt. 2 passes to 3, 1 or 5.

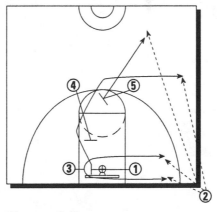

Diagram 9-18.

Because this play generally does not create immediate scoring opportunities, your players must get into an offense once the ball is inbounded. Instead of setting up and running a set play, we immediately organize into one of our breakdown offenses, detailed in Chapters 6 and 7.

INBOUNDING ON THE SIDELINE

Inbounding the ball on the sideline represents the middle ground between optimal position on the baseline and difficult territory in the corner. In general, it is easier to inbound from the sideline than from the corner. Therefore, it makes sense to run a set play with scoring options, rather than creating only outlets, then immediately getting into a breakdown offense once the ball is inbounded.

Play No. 16
My personal favorite in this situation is a set play that creates a variety of inside and outside options. It employs a series of screens and ball and player movement; choreographed, but with options. This frees your players to take advantage of indecision or poor judgment by defenders.

Diagram 9-19: 5 and 1 line up on the ball side. 5 screens down for 1—the ideal big-for-small screen. 3 inbounds to 1.

Diagram 9-20: 4 and 5 set separate screens for 3, creating isolation for 2 on the weak side. 1 passes the ball to 2 on the opposite wing. 2 has the option of a backdoor cut if he is overplayed. If 2 catches the ball on the wing, he looks inside for 3, cutting off a screen by either 4 or 5 to the low block.

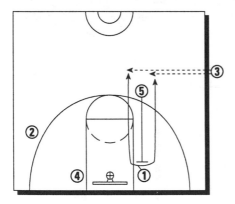

Diagram 9-19.

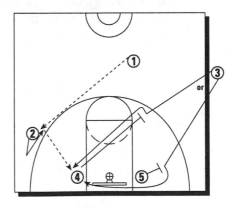

Diagram 9-20.

Diagram 9-21: Suppose that 1 is overplayed on the initial cut. Instead of coming up the lane as an initial outlet, 1 breaks to the ballside corner for a pass from 3. 4 cuts diagonally to the ballside elbow area.

Diagram 9-22: On the continuation of this action, 1 dribbles to a high wing area. 4 screens for 3. 1 lobs to 3 for a layup or short pull-up shot.

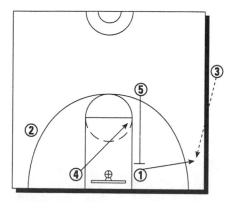

Diagram 9-21.

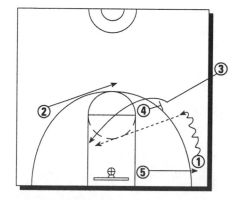

Diagram 9-22.

John Kresse is director of athletics and men's basketball coach at the College of Charleston. During Kresse's first 19 seasons at the College of Charleston, his teams compiled a 465-118 record, a .798 winning percentage. From 1994 through 1998, Kresse's teams won 125 games, five straight Trans America Athletic Conference regular-season championships, and the TAAC post-season tournament in 1997 and 1998. That success led to a string of five post-season appearances (three NCAA, two NIT), including an NIT victory over Tennessee in 1996 and an opening-round NCAA Tournament victory over Maryland in 1997. After defeating Maryland, the College of Charleston took eventual national champion Arizona to the final seconds before losing, 73-69, in the second round. The College of Charleston finished the 1997 season with a 29-3 record, ranked 16th in the final Associated Press poll and 21st in the final CNN-USA Today poll.

Earlier in Kresse's tenure, the College of Charleston won the NAIA championship in 1983 and placed third nationally in 1988. From 1960 through 1979, Kresse played for and coached with Joe Lapchick and Lou Carnesecca at St. John's University and with the New York Nets of the American Basketball Association.

Richard Jablonski is a Research Associate at the Medical University of South Carolina, assistant basketball coach at Trident Academy in Mount Pleasant, SC, and television analyst of College of Charleston basketball. From 1979 through 1988, he was a reporter and columnist for newspapers in New York and South Carolina. His coverage of the College of Charleston's NAIA championship basketball team in 1983 earned first-place honors in the South Carolina Press Association's annual competition. From 1988 through 1993, Jablonski served as play-by-play voice or analyst on the College of Charleston Radio Network.

ADDITIONAL BASKETBALL
RESOURCES FROM

COACHES CHOICE

- ***ATTACKING ZONE DEFENSES (2nd Ed.)***
  by John Kresse and Richard Jablonski
  1997 ▪ Paper ▪ 128 pp
  ISBN 1-57167-047-5 ▪ $16.95

- ***COACHING FAST BREAK BASKETBALL (2nd Ed.)***
  by Cliff Ellis
  1997 ▪ Paper ▪ 142 pp
  ISBN 1-57167-158-7 ▪ $16.95 each

- ***ZONE PRESS VARIATIONS FOR WINNING BASKETBALL (2nd Ed.)***
  by Cliff Ellis
  1997 ▪ Paper ▪ 104 pp
  ISBN 1-57167-159-5 ▪ $16.95 each

- ***101 WOMEN'S BASKETBALL DRILLS***
  by Theresa Grentz and Gary Miller
  1997 ▪ Paper ▪ 128 pp
  ISBN 1-57167-083-1 ▪ $16.95